May the Grace of God
Be Multiplied to you!
Shalom
Delmelodia Tipton

AuthorHouse™
1663 Liberty Drive
Bloomington, IN 47403
www.authorhouse.com
Phone: 1 (800) 839-8640

Published by AuthorHouse 04/10/2018

ISBN: 978-1-5462-2932-2 (sc)
ISBN: 978-1-5462-2931-5 (e)

Library of Congress Control Number: 2018902053

Scripture taken from The Holy Bible, King James Version. Public Domain

New International Version (NIV)
Holy Bible, New International Version®, NIV® Copyright ©1973, 1978, 1984, 2011 by Biblica, Inc.® Used by permission. All rights reserved worldwide.

Amplified Bible (AMP)
Copyright © 2015 by The Lockman Foundation, La Habra, CA 90631. All rights reserved.

Holman Christian Standard Bible (HCSB)
Copyright © 1999, 2000, 2002, 2003, 2009 by Holman Bible Publishers, Nashville Tennessee. All rights reserved.

International Standard Version (ISV)
Copyright © 1995-2014 by ISV Foundation. ALL RIGHTS RESERVED INTERNATIONALLY. Used by permission of Davidson Press, LLC.

Image Logo Artist: Rasheda Davis
Website: www.bvpllc.biz

FORGIVEN
BREAK THE CHAIN

Yeshua Ha-Mashiach

Ambassadors4Christ

Delmelodia Tipton

authorHOUSE®

DEDICATED TO YOU!
REVIVAL IN THE LAND OF THE SOUL!!

With promises like this to pull us on, dear friends, let's make a clean break with everything that defiles or distracts us, both within and without. Let's make (through the blood of Yeshua) our entire lives fit and holy temples for the worship (reverence) of God.
2 CORINTHIANS 7:1 (MSG)

ENDORSEMENTS

Wow! A must read for the True Body of Christ and all Elohim's creation seeking "Knowledge and Understanding" shown through his agape "Forgiven and Freedom" toward us; then, extend it out from our hearts to others. Come and walk in his forgiveness that causes chains to break. Allow the Lord Jesus Christ to free you in all areas that have kept you in bondage.

Prophetess Iliana Pratcher
TBOC (The Body of Christ) MINISTRIES

Elder Delmelodia Tipton gives us a complete study guide of the mystery work of the cross concerning Forgiven "Break The Chain." This work reminds us that the greatest victory that anyone can achieve is to be able to walk in freedom. This teaching shows how the work that began at Calvary when Jesus died on the cross to set us free releases the anointing to break chains. As you read this study resource you will receive great insight along with scripture reference throughout this book. I recommend this book for new Christians, as well as, those who have been in the Christian faith for many years.

Dr. Roosevelt T. Joyner
Koinonia Baptist Church

We are propelled to recognize who we are, what we know to believe and ultimately how we choose to respond. We can choose to become imprisoned and tormented or we can choose to labor to find peace, calm, rest and confidently trust in God's unconditional love and treasures through the Finished Work of the CROSS. In this Book, "Forgiven", Elder Delmelodia Tipton, *whom I have grown to know as my sister in Christ, "Mel"*, masterfully, *through personal traumatic experiences*, expounds in this manual and teaches readers the way of freedom. In John 14:20, Jesus tells us (paraphrased), He is in the Father, we are in Him, and He is in us. Look at our God!!!! It is my prayer that each reader allows every God inspired page of "Forgiven" to minister through every area of life and encourage you; by doing so, WE ARE THE TRIUMPHANT CHURCH IN CHRIST. God Bless!!!!

Minister Paula T. Rankins
A Servant in Christ
World Overcomers Outreach Ministries Church

ABOUT THE AUTHOR

Delmelodia Tipton is a Spirit-filled woman of God, woman of faith and prayer, intercessor, entrepreneur, author, mother of two daughters and the wife of David Tipton. This is her third revelatory teaching manual inspired under the directions, insight and wisdom of the Holy Spirit. The woman of God is cloaked with a mantle and spiritual gifts ordained from the backside of the wilderness and through the refinery Hand of God. The Lord has summon, trained, anointed and appointed her to preach and flow in the capacity of his anointing for the purposes of soul deliverance and equipping souls to walk in their priestly position. She has served faithfully over the years under the apostolic leadership of Apostle Larry (Iliana) Pratcher Jr. Delmelodia Tipton teaches from the Hebraic faith which is the root of the body of Christ salvation in Yeshua (Jesus). Delmelodia Tipton is host and founder of Ambassadors 4Christ Apostolic Telecast Ministry commissioned to reach, teach and preach the Word of God to the nations. To become a kingdom sponsor or partner by sowing financially to support the Kingdom of God mission work in the earth, visit the website @ www.ambassaduer4christ.net.

FOREWORD

I believe as you not only read this teaching, but study and ponder that God will awaken your spiritual senses to the deeper realities in him. I am privileged as an author to write from my experiences which the Hand of God has guided me through to release the increase of Yahweh's wisdom to you. As I hear the voice of the Lord and understand the insight, I'm humbled to share with you the word of knowledge and divine revelation. It amazes me to see the strength of God; his plans, assignments, love and purpose he has ordained for the body of Christ... his Bride. I believe approaching seasons are being stirred to arouse the body of Christ concerning God's omnipotence and our position. I certainly have seen the Hand of God and the power of his breathe speak in situations that concerns me; not only am I still standing, but I testify that I live, move and have my being in Jesus. I testify as a witness that God is doing immeasurably above all that we can imagine or ask according to His Holy Spirit that works... seek him. I testify by his blood that his love, his...compassion, his anointing and his glory is a reality. And I bear witness that as you set quality time aside to indulge in this manual that your understanding will be increased. Holy Spirit is doing a continual and sustaining work. All that He does for one He's sure to do for another. He shows no favoritism. No matter how it may look, I encourage your heart to hold on to God in faith because only the Spirit of God knows the course of this divine faith journey. Indulge with readiness to receive. May the blessings of godly wisdom, strength and peace be multiplied through this great work in Christ Jesus toward you.

Woman of God,
Delmelodia Tipton

PREFACE

The Spirit of the LORD revealed a vision to me during a worship service. The praise and worship was high and the Presence of the LORD spoke expressively in song, prophetically and demonstratively. Holy Spirit took me in the spirit and I saw what looked like a film or fog in the atmosphere in the sanctuary… His angel of Presence and Glory was there ready to release divine counsel, fresh anointing, fire that heals, fire that breaks/ sever ungodly yokes and manifests deliverance in the heart. The CROSS is the picture of eternal love, salvation, sacrifice, obedience, forgiveness and freedom. Forgiven relates personally between you and the Savior that carries you throughout your walk of salvation. Forgiveness, a spiritual matter of the heart and divine union, is also an action that is toward others from the power of the Godhead and commanded to be personally extended from you toward another. Forgiven (ness) is the redemption act that obliterates all manner of spiritual oppression of the soul. Even in the Church, the accuser of the brethren still operates to infiltrate and incarcerate the mind and soul through dishonest (lies) persuasions that sound right to the thought which creates behavior; starting outwardly gaining led way for control into the inward chambers of the heart. The Church is authorized to overcome such persuasion, but in order to overcome such bondage the Church (Ekklesia) must recognize the reality of the Power of the CROSS. This revelation…birthed the understanding of freedom from the start and to the completion of this teaching manual. We relate salvation to a once in a life time experience; however, that one time experience is the supernatural entrance of God's Kingdom into our spirit to restructure and teach the redeemed of the LORD how to live and function as citizens of the Kingdom of GOD sphere of influence in the earth realm. The New Covenant exhibits a kingdom bloodline that is supernatural which calls for supernatural maintenance through submission and agreement. Because ABBA cares for His children; His children are commanded to run into him for safety. Supernatural safety that provides supernatural strength, power, covering, wisdom and Holy Ghost fire against falling away, reverting and conforming to worldly concepts or the sinful nature. God exposes the enemies of our soul and secures our freedom and future by breaking every chain that seeks to bind us up. When one is bound in any way or form bondage works restriction against a believer's identity, position and activation. Bondage opposes freedom's manifestations. Forgiven grace is the divine love that called us from the grave to a new life of experiencing freedom in Christ. Forgiven and freedom are one bond, like love and mercy co-existing, together. The CROSS frees souls from all debt and all indictments that will rise in the future. The soul is forgiven, set free through the Power of the Blood of Yeshua (Jesus) that prevails over all that will oppose us in this lifetime.

The LORD desires a sacrificial worship offering from your heart to His... a holy offering on the altar unto him. The Spirit of the LORD will add the fire. The Fire, His Presence, the Glory of the LORD is what consumes the guilt, the pretending, the idols, fear, emotionalism and formalism and carries purity to the heart, mind and manner of life. True revival starts in the heart with GOD and spreads like fire... our life is to be a sacrifice before the LORD; naked... heart bear... Here Am I, LORD. When GOD comes in the midst, His Presence and Glory have what you are in need of... authorized fire that unlocks and disband constraints, weights, torture off the soul and mind, and emotions. That which incarcerates the mind is arrested in His Holy Presence and Glory. That unwarranted, illegal spirit that work through people in the church, families, household, on jobs or campus to bring fear, harm or witchcraft against the believer is consumed by the Fire of GOD... set free. It is in the Presence of the LORD that the worshiper is covered, cleansed, strengthen, mind empowered, newness overshadows and vision cloaks the worshiper's soul. The LORD revealed that it's His standard of Holiness and FIRE hoisted against temptation, every wayward association, every fiery arrow and every evil work against His Body... the Church. Although it forms No WEAPON shall prosper and every idle word is brought into judgment by the LORD Himself. It may form, but shall not prosper against those that worship in Spirit and Truth. The LORD revealed this as another demonstrative operation of His forgiveness working FREEDOM; unlocking what is mentally chained up, deliverance for the soul and body... freeing those who are incarcerated and overruling what challenges or speaks contrary to the Word of GOD... and consistency and persistently engaging in pure worship.

Chains are like a fortified fortress that holds a soul hostage to its territory with or without the soul's permission. In other words, it is a diabolic force of interference that attempts to imprint its darkness upon the soul and mind in order to keep one from their created divine purpose in Christ. Being chained up begins from a seed-thought sown in the heart or mind; conceived through unsanctioned emotions and affections which have been or are being channeled in another pathway opposite of the Truth through doors pertaining to the past exposing itself in the present; with an extreme appetite to kill, steal and destroy purpose and the image of God. Often times in life one's heart can become bruised, callous, confused or bounded from issues that seem not to go away or the residue of circumstances that seem to keep resurfacing over and over again or circumstances that dictate strongly that this is the way life is suppose to be. Such issue(s) that form in one's personal life can be powerful enough to redirect one's course, lock up one's mind and heart to block Truth and retard spiritual growth in Christ. This causes bondage and is sabotage from within. Although extended issues can form from decisions, we personally play a part in allowing moody forces of persuasion form from within penetrating its dark power for controlling you and your destiny. Chains are broken off your life and off your mind when one makes the faith move to bow to the LORD and divorce -fall out of agreement- with ungodly resistance, falsehood, its' way of thinking, its' persuasion and its' family of lies. Instead of allowing it to push you back, rise in the authority of the Word of God and push it back. The Church is to see it for what it is through the wisdom of the Spirit of GOD. This spiritual restraint will challenge the imagination, emotions and the weakness of the flesh.

Bondage blinds spiritual eyes and ears and distances the heart from wholesomeness. Bondage, like a chain of deadly toxin, holds a soul in prison and alienated from grace virtues, the Presence and Glory of Yahweh in Christ. Today, many experience vexation, spiritual depression or despair and spiritual slumber that can only be spiritually discerned and overcome by the Power of the Finished Work of the CROSS. The selfless obedient act of Jesus authorizes a believer supernaturally from within to resist and overcome the work of such persuasions, the cunningness of impure emotions and authority to walk in freedom grace. The Grace of Forgiven that sets us free... breaks covenant with the old, the past, in order to set us free to receive the new and flourish in the promised life through liberation of the spirit and mind. The old spiritual agreement is nullified through the Blood of Jesus; quashed, abolished or made invalid through the CROSS. The perfecting work of Jesus Christ is the answer for every soul today and for all eternity. The divine imprint of holy righteousness reads "FORGIVEN." All which once held us captive in mind, spirit, heart, soul, body and deed is now captive through the Power of CROSS... libration of the soul and life in the Spirit.

Forgiveness works toward us for us to work toward others, even if they do not receive it. Mercy presents itself at the cost of you denying yourself. Forgiveness puts the soul that is initiating the very act in a different sphere than the soul that rejects its work… sphere of light and sphere of darkness. Understanding the function of forgiven and its parallel relation to the CROSS and the soul helps you understand what is and is not ordained by GOD. Divine forgiveness is the power that involves the removal of stains surface deep. The Blood is the only power that removes such blemishes and leaves no traces; our deliverance is at the CROSS. This book will teach, guide and open your understanding in a broader perspective of the Power of the CROSS. The believer has been given a royal seat in Christ, authority to release, identification and the power to overcome illegal repressions, break its vision and uproot its seed by the Word of GOD, the Fire of the Holy Spirit and submission. GOD is a yoke destroyer. He desires for every single soul to be free from all chains of bondage and to walk in that knowledge of liberty. No matter what the chain is Yeshua (Jesus) paid the price for our freedom that provided complete deliverance. Understanding the finished work of the CROSS releases Kingdom graces that belong to believers as heirs through Christ Jesus. Forgiven is the grace dimension to step forward through acceptance and submission from that which once held us captive. When a soul steps into this realm the outlook is new and divinely renewed with Logos (The WORD-Yeshua) knowledge and through the Power of Ruach Hakodesh (Holy Spirit). Choose to be free. Each time a thought attitude appears to bring bondage, hold your mind in prison and hold you chained to the past (mind control-witchcraft)… by the Power of GOD, "Command that Chain to Break in Yeshua's (Jesus) Name!!!" I Prophesy That You Step Forward, STEP Out! DON'T HESITATE!!! DON'T RETHINK IT! MOVE SWIFTLY! GUARD YOUR MIND In The WORD And STEP!!! Step into That Dimension of total freedom; the supernatural and natural reality of what is real to the royal priesthood in Christ Jesus.

Forgiven is every believer in Christ grace endorsement and the Kingdom of Yahweh in Christ never-ending victory extension of action. Although forgiven is timeless…eternal, it is a godly practice of grace to be demonstrated through each believing soul. What the CROSS accomplished and the grave had no power to hold is to be exhibited by faith in the new life of the redeemed. Forgiven is a holy principle expressed through genuine agape that's entwined in the essence and character of Yeshua (Jesus). Forgiven is Yahweh (GOD the Father) action of sovereignty releasing His holiness, justice, holy conviction, acquittal -freedom- and love toward all humanity. Forgiven course of action liberates the believer's soul completely from guilt and shame; our past and translated us as new creatures in Christ into the dimension of the new and real…old things are past away and all things are made new. This liberation carries a supernatural transformation which takes place in the soul by the work of Holy Spirit. This new dimension and liberation is unknown to all that pertains to the old pathway and old thought. **The Bible tells us in [Colossians 1:13-14] For He rescued us from the dominion of darkness and brought us into the kingdom of the Son He loves, in whom we have redemption, the forgiveness of sins.** Yeshua (Jesus) is JEHOVAH-TSIDKENU, the LORD our Righteousness. Yeshua stripped and dismantled the authority and power of the evil one that once legally owned our soul through the power of salvation. Now the soul is in the spiritual process for renewal by the power of the Holy Spirit. Divine forgiveness and forgiven transcends every evil act of incrimination, darkness, familiar spirits, perversion, curses, hostility, accusations, iniquity and transgression. Although all this is presently manifested in this earthly sphere, the wisdom of the LORD overrules its' authority and power through infinite love, infinite favor, infinite victory and infinite peace through Christ.

We can witness this demonstration for all of mankind and for all times at our Savior's crucifixion at Calvary: the two criminals on their cross and the declaration Jesus (Yeshua) spoke as He hung in severe violent, excruciating agonizing pain from the fogging, the nails and the spear piercing His side. **The Bible tells us in [Luke 23:39-43] One of the criminals who hung there hurled insults at Him: Aren't you the Messiah: Save yourself and us. But the other criminal rebuked him. Don't you fear God, he said, since you are under the same sentence? We are punished justly, for we are getting what our deeds deserve. But this man has done nothing wrong. Then he said, Yeshua remember me when you come into your kingdom. Jesus answered him, Truly I tell you, today you will be with me in paradise.** The twofold act of grace and mercy is demonstrated toward all people that will humble... the lost (degenerated) and the backslider that has fallen. Forgiven grace act reveals Yeshua's eternal authority and power to blot out sin and cancel the eternal death transaction; removing all charges that lead to execution by the death penalty... "FORGIVEN" by grace through faith with a reward of eternity with Him in paradise. Forgiven grace cancels out all that enslaves or have an effect on us through mental bondage, emotional bondage, generational bondage, history bondage, economic bondage and physical bondage... spiritual bondage reinforced by the spirit of sabotage. The CROSS not only provided the way of God's Kingdom, our citizenship and righteousness, but also released the way for believers in Christ to walk in kingdom dominion in the earth.

Forgiven although it deals with our past and the finished sealed work of the CROSS, its virtue extends to the present time to any soul that have a change of heart to turn from that which seeks to bring captivity. This mercy act brings the heart into a profitable way of life with GOD by the power of the Holy Spirit and the Blood of JESUS. It's the power of GOD that rests, rules and dwells. Forgiven mercy act, like a bill of right, activates complete deliverance for all responding souls. It's granted, supplied and supported by GOD alone. We can't say or claim we have GOD without accepting the complete work of the CROSS; the life, death, burial and the resurrection of Jesus (Yeshua). We can't say we have the Father or claim Yeshua and deny the perfecting work of the Spirit of GOD (Holy Spirit) who is the demonstrator of the power of salvation and glory. We can't say we have the Father and Jesus as Savior; yet, deny the active power of the resurrection and the active power of Holy Spirit in the earth today through the Church. The sacrificial act of remission is the foundation in the glorified work of the manifested Glory of the begotten Son of GOD, Yeshua; justification and spiritual acquittal. The Redemption and Remission Act through way of the bloody CROSS, Christ our Mediator, removed the repentant who was a criminal of the state out of the place of eternal condemnation and totally erases the penalty charged…all pending charges for the crimes. The crime of sin and rebellion against GOD within the heart incriminates the soul. Jesus Christ took the penalty for the charge that stood against Father GOD justice and holiness; the execution that you and I so rightly deserved. God's Justice System stood up and stooped to rescue us. Mercy and truth join together and righteousness and peace kissed **[Psalm 85:10]**.

God's grace operates to extend His holiness. Jesus sealed every wound we would experience in in His body…sealed every affliction imaginable in His body to reunite GOD and man through the buy back payment… the natural with the supernatural and to put the souls that confess back in proper rank. The Gift of Everlasting life provides the Church with righteousness to experience in this life and to share in spiritual blessings as heirs of GOD. **The Bible tells us in [Isaiah 53:5-6] But He (Yeshua) was wounded for our transgressions; he was bruised for our iniquities: the chastisement of our peace was upon him; and with his stripes we are healed. All we like sheep have gone astray; we have turned, every one to his own way; and the LORD has laid on Him (Jesus) the iniquity of us all.** He bore our wounds and bruises in His body. Every act for healing and deliverance was accomplished in JESUS 39 stripes. All that pertain to our healing and all that pertain to our deliverance in this life... daily bread, heaven to earth, is brought about in the 39 lashes... freedom's inheritance. Yeshua's (Jesus) blood met the judgment for every infirmity of mind, body, heart, bloodline... shortcomings, grief and sorrows. Think about that! His Peace! His Love! Justice lifted up our heads and arms manifesting Jesus Glory over defeat. He turned His face to the Father for you and I to partake of grace to be made whole inside first and then outwardly. Jesus said, I'll go, Father, prepare me a body **[Hebrew 10:5]**. And through His body and blood He gave the more excellent way of liberation in order for the believer rule in the power of Holy Spirit and to enter into His Presence. Jesus is the difference against all odds. Forgiven breaks every chain declaring the state of freedom...a public declaration. Freedom is united to humility, loyalty and dependence upon the LORD of Covenant...Redeemer, Judge, Master and King.

As we have the understanding of the foundation of the physical Constitution of Rights and the system then, the body of Christ (Ekklesia) can compare its liveliness and energy in understanding the divine Constitution (covenant) of the Kingdom of GOD. This is the divine bill of legitimate birth right through adoption and the Power of the Blood of Jesus; and the eternal governmental system... Yahweh, Yeshua, Ruach Hakodesh. The Church has grasped no doubt that believers are reborn, redeemed or regenerated through the work of the Spirit of GOD through grace by faith. However, the Law of the Spirit of Christ that gives us new life actually gives us life in the Spirit and summons the Church (believers) to be spiritual and holy; functioning from a different dimension in the grace of GOD while in the earth. The Lord's provision of redemption emancipation extends to our body, as well as, to the soul: the will, emotions, desires, intellect, thoughts and affections. Our character, personality, nature or persona is a representation of what's living within the soul. As we recognize and walk in redemption full knowledge, Truth and godly wisdom, not only will the Church win every battle every time, but the Church will be well inform, spiritually far-sighted and on one accord with eternities strength. Spiritually inclined to see, hear and built up with a clothed mind and heart not to shrink back into spiritual captivity (slavery)...frame of mind, persuasion of thinking.

The Ekklesia (Body of Christ) is called to mature spiritually to see bondage as GOD sees it, see freedom as GOD sees it, see sin as GOD sees it, to see grace as GOD sees it, see elevation as GOD sees it, see obedience as GOD sees it, see the future as GOD sees it and to see eternal things as GOD sees them. Because this is supernatural it functions according to the measure of divine power that works within the believer...Holy Ghost power. Ruach Hakodesh (Holy Spirit) divine revelation brings transformation, healing and deliverance to any thirsty soul. The soul that is thirsty is open to receive correction, patience, self control and guidance to live purposefully. This is vital to our advancement because where Light is darkness will flee. When the Ruach (Spirit) of the LORD shines the Light he exposes darkness, weakness and lack in any form to breathe afresh a new atmosphere, a new direction, a new persuasion, a new vision, new strength, new behavior, new love and new insight that's in accordance with His Kingdom sphere of influence. Holy Spirit purposely rewires the soul, sort of speak, by divine Light which darkness cannot comprehend nor remain. Yahweh's salvation can be described in these stages: 1) underserved favor 2) justification 3) sanctification 4) Holy Ghost infilling 5) purging or deliverance 6) inheritance transfer and 7) glorification. Forgiven is the garment of amazing grace that establishes divine intention in the present. For a moment, view forgiven grace through its function, eternal freedom for the soul (like the Bill of Rights: individual freedom rights, protection for the citizens of that nation; therefore, in the eternal system the Bill of Right is the Blood of Jesus). This comparison will help to understand the depths of "Forgiven Grace" regulation of GOD...for continuous spiritual perfection in Christ and transitioning as we occupy in this land. Forgiven, the divine constitution, meets the holy standard of divine righteousness against all forms of incrimination and harmful effects of sin; turning everything right side up in order to release the decrees of King Jesus. Because of forgiven grace supernatural virtues, gifts, crowns and mantles are inherited through the blood...atoning sacrifice of the LORD JESUS CHRIST...satisfying the holy justice of Yahweh the Father.

Remember, forgiven is the transcending wisdom of the Power of the CROSS that cancels out defeat in all of its appearances and accusations against the believer that lay ahead, decapitates the head of our enemies and releases divine justice...teardown every high altar, break every chain and every yoke. Freedom in Christ confirms the shift that is supernatural. Liberty in Christ changes the believer's outlook and zone because the life is Christ; and the life that is Christ is made perfect and righteous by way of His blood covenant **[Romans 3:21-22]**. Again, the life hidden in Christ becomes His life, the Word, living through you. You are made perfect (mature) by the life of the living and active Word. This perfection relates to our mind and behavior in Christ. Your hands, mouth and body becomes His dwelling for demonstration and usage. This perfection of maturity is found only in Christ Jesus...non other. Therefore, you and I are chosen by Him to be perfect (spiritual maturity) even before the foundation of the world **[Ephesians 1:4]** as our Father is perfect **[Matthew 5:48]**; not by our strength, thought or mental power, but by His wisdom and thought. **The Bible tells us in [Psalm 19:7] The Law of the LORD is perfect, restoring the soul; the testimony of the LORD is sure, making wise the simple.** The Law of the LORD is the believer's foundation and inborn inheritance for favor made through the finished work of the CROSS. The Law of the LORD develops the believer value of living, understanding and judgment. The Law is Christ. The Law is the Spirit. The Law is the Word no separation; one strength, one wisdom, one Spirit, one domain and one purpose...to instruct and govern...breaking every shackle of bondage. That's the compassion and long suffering of His grace from the beginning to the end.

We understand that Jesus paid the price for the soul's freedom and birthright. The justice of Jesus blood extends grace to our faculties, too; our heart, our thought capacity and desires...making them anew by adding Himself to those areas; in adding and increasing Himself, Yeshua (Jesus) perfects that which is imperfect and flawed. The blood of Yeshua is the supernatural blend of His soul and breath... one Spirit. There is an old song verse that says, "His Blood Reaches to the Lowest Valley" and that valley is the soul of mankind. As life happens we need the blood to speak in the midst of whatever is taking place. Just as bad company can corrupt good character, trying times can corrupt good character as well. Although both situations may be a test and experienced through the course of life for learning, hearts must be equipped with the statues of the LORD. When His Word is written on the table of the heart it combats the corruption and temptation that waits at the door of the heart in such times to place a burden upon the mind and a yoke on the neck. However, due to the blood being alive, each Spirit-filled believer is qualified and empowered to speak to the situation for a reverse action through knowing and obeying the Word. Because of the worthiness Christ paid on the CROSS, the divine constitution of GOD...the Blood of Jesus, is the only power of authority to crush that which comes to crush you. In view of the truth the Blood of Jesus is the New Covenant that redeems and increase spiritual consciousness to cause spiritual soberness in the mind, heart and soul.

Every evil tongue or thought that lied to you and caused harm Jesus Commands it to be crushed by the power of His Blood and the authority of His Name. Every blood pact, spirit of racism, spirit of suicide, spirit of depression, strong willed, covetousness, adulterous, fornication, murderous, bitter, envy, spiteful, resentful, spirit of infirmity, hatred, rebellious spirit and Jim Crow enslavement... JESUS COMMANDS THE CHAINS TO BREAK NOW OFF YOUR MIND! BE CRUSHED! BE HEALED by the Power of the finished work of the CROSS; the Blood Potency! The LORD Commands the residue to evaporate. Such manifestations are already judged by the Spirit of GOD for the believer to counterattack in the realm of the spirit with the Word; freedom's divine manifestation through the work of salvation. The Power of the finish work of the CROSS gives the Church power to overcome such tyrants. Ask yourself this question, "Am I walking in my GOD given liberty...is my soul free, is my mind free, are my emotions free, is my body free?" GOD will move when the heart looks unto Him...although He sees it, we must release our heart location to receive divine grace activations and manifestations [**Proverbs 18:14**]. Exponential growth, effectiveness and divine power are declared to be the believer's reality today.

Forgiven grace relation is entwined as one work force. The soul that is saved reveals the washing by the blood for the remissions of sin...eternal salvation. The Spirit of Christ now abides in the human spirit of the believer as the indwelling Light of rebirth. The souls' persecutor, satan, will still seek to bring up charges to wreck the believer in Christ. **The Bible tells us in [Galatians 5:1] It is**

for freedom that Christ has set us free. Stand firm then and do not be entangled, burdened again with the yoke of slavery. The soul is ready to experience a life of freedom through healing and transformation from the infusion of the CROSS. The believer must protect their new heritage in all life matters. One of the duties of Holy Spirit is to fill up the premises of the spiritual house (new man) with a new level of obedience and a new knowledge of the LORD which are very important to our new walk. The Ruach (Spirit) of GOD is the Church teacher and advocate of the new soul and the new nature. Since the spirit is now reconciled to the Master, GOD benefits include total restoration; grace virtue that carries weight and volume in the spirit realm and the natural realm by the Holy Spirit. This restoration depends on and requires the perfecting Hand of GOD. All which once plagued your soul will attempt to return and introduce a mix point of view. Don't Be Deceived! Don't Be Delayed and Don't Get Stuck! Come into complete agreement with the Word of GOD for your destiny. The finished work of the CROSS lives to express its completeness throughout our lives which reveals that God's Spirit is actively doing a continuous perfecting work within us **[Philippians 1:6]** through submission. The believer's spiritual state is restored through the CROSS, all bondage is only abolished through the CROSS and triumph is rewarded through the CROSS Death, Burial and Resurrection of JESUS. Those who are restored spiritually will see manifestations in their life. The CROSS accomplished our deliverance, inheritance and future hope; the covenant for freedom to be established personally. However, we wrestle spiritually against that which seeks to oppress us and steal our freedom. Freedom in Christ positions the mind of those that faithfully indulge themselves to excel above the realm of stagnation and imperfection; seeing through the vision of the CROSS.

No matter what we have done the Blood of Jesus cleanses the soul and throws the sin and its' bondage in the sea. This means offenders are ex-offenders released from all past guilt, all negligence; as if we had never ever committed the crime...sit back, reflect on your life and in every door absorb and meditate on that Truth. The Blood of Jesus is the covenant that releases the promises and without the shedding of holy blood there is no inheritance, no freedom, no remission, no covenant, no favor, no grace, no peace and no forgiveness [**Hebrew 9:22**]: *Aphiemi Greek word for forgiven means separation, put off, total detachment.* Forgiven grace works on behalf of the criminal of the state at salvation and on behalf of the Church continuously [**1 John 1:7**]. This is called the passing over, the remittal for the consequences of the penalty of sin which brings on spiritual sleep, death, bondage, spiritual division and eternal separation. The blood sanctions those of faith into the realm of the new...all things are made new. That is literary leaving nothing untouched "All Things" from the heart...motives, from the finances to marriage intimacy, etc. The blood is the security for the healing and identity of the Church in Christ. The word remission comes from two Greek words: *1. Aphesis means send away, forgive, release or pardon 2. Paresis means pass over, to have compassion for; parallel in function with the Hebrew word pesach which means and relates to pass through, exempt, to spare and Passover* [**Exodus 12:12-13; 23:15; John 13:1-3**]. This points to the Lamb of GOD who was slain to take away the sins of the world [**John 1:29**]; to bring liberation from bondage, alienation and hostility. Regardless of how the laws of the land change...physical laws...the Law of GOD will never compromise or change to accommodate mankind pleasures, rejection or rebellion. God's Law Is Law...Covenant with Himself. Yeshua declares, I Am the New Covenant this is my blood and my body, take and eat [**Matthew 26:26-27; Luke 22:19-20**] the Passover Lamb of Yahweh [**1 Corinthians 11:24-25**]...that which is already done to guarantee eternal peace and safety (restoration, communion and fellowship); the seal of the New Covenant by the Spirit of GOD. The perfect life of Jesus and His blood is the Gate for GOD and man to come into covenant agreement and cancel the old contract and bring in the new. JESUS is the Mediator -go between- of the New Covenant...the Lawyer for the removal of the sinful appetite; freedom from imprisonment and cleansing of the conscience. **The Bible tells us in [Jeremiah 31:33] This is the covenant I will make with the people of Israel after that time, declares the LORD. I will put my law in their minds and write it on their hearts. I will be their God and they will be my people. [Hebrew 10:16] This is the covenant I will make with them after that time says the Lord. I will put my laws in their hearts and I will write them on their minds.** Remember, the actions of a new level of obedience, a new level of knowledge of the Lord, a new heart and a new mind are birthed through the grace promise of the New Covenant...new level, new dimension(s). God's covenant applies to every soul that partakes; not to a sex, race, custom or nationality of people, but whosoever will...Come, I will renew a right spirit and free your soul. Now the believer in Christ in the royal family can experience daily renewal and new mercies daily...covenant promises. As we understand Truth as a privilege, we must then "will" to apply it in every area of our lives: personally, emotionally, physically, spiritually, marriage, singles, divorced, work place, prayer, business, entertainment, school, ambition, financially, socially and privately...no secret doors. All that does not belong to the believer shall be dethroned and deliverance will come to the heart and soul.

A divine covenant is unlike a contract (which has an end date) its divine purpose is to never end. The covenant involves uniting one party with another through agreement with the Head of the covenant of power or the superior to the inferior... a supernatural betweenness that unites two as one. GOD brings believers into an expected end that entails oneness, benefits, penalties, character and responsibilities through His covenant for establishing His Kingdom on earth as it is in heaven [**Matthew 6:10**]. *Covenant comes from the Hebrew word Beriyth which means covenant treaty or binding agreement between two parties.* A covenant is a permanent arrangement and involves the totality of who you are to become by the power source of it; like a marriage covenant. A covenant has visible signs which represent the agreement. The physical marriage union which is ordained by GOD to demonstrate acts of loyalty, friendship, oneness, agreement, trustworthiness, fidelity, openness, commitment, accountability, love, time, patience and mercy. This is the pattern example of what the spiritual Covenant of GOD already is and more. Covenant is the constitution signed, sealed and delivered in the Blood of Yeshua. When GOD makes covenant to bless His people in return the people are to show signs of faithfulness and to serve as a channel toward others… just as He did with Abraham, Noah, Adam, Moses and David. Faithfulness on our part is a form of worship and loyalty revealed through our lifestyle; a virtue, a constant learning, training and maturity in the covenant of grace and is not to be taken for granted. Faithfulness is to be evident on the earth at the second coming of Christ [**Luke 18:8; 1 Thessalonians 4:14-17**]. The covenant of favor complete work through the Blood of Jesus, a sign sealed for the believers' redemption once for all times, is the promise that guarantees GOD as the covenant keeper of covenant blessings.

GOD calls the heart to dine in sincerity as citizens of His Kingdom authorizing us to walk in dominion and authority especially in times of affliction and hardship. **The Bible tells us in [Proverbs 8:14] Counsel is mine and sound wisdom: I am understanding; I have strength.** The wisdom of GOD teaches and influences us how to live through circumstances that challenges us to maintain confidence in Him. **The Bible tells us in [Proverbs 11:14] Where no counsel is, the people fall, but in the multitude** of counselors there is safety... good advise. The Bible tells us in [Proverbs 20:5] Counsel in the heart of man is like deep water, but a man of understanding will draw it out. GOD invites the soul to come reason together in His courtroom, on His terms and by His measuring rod. Consider! Come with your heart, deeds, thoughts and concerns and place them before the righteous Judge in all of His wisdom and might. Come! Walk with me (the Lord), abide and my (the Lord) Kingdom will abide in you. Its' GOD supernatural transaction and deposit into dust; a deposit of His glory in earthen vessels [2 Corinthians 4:7]. The wisdom of the LORD is the power of right reasoning and there is security to all who draw from Him. The Bible tells us in [Ephesians 3:16-19] I pray that out of his glorious riches he may strengthen you with power through his Spirit in your inner being, so that Christ may dwell in your hearts through faith. And I pray that you, being rooted and established in love, may have power together with all the Lord's holy people, to grasp how wide and long and high and deep is the love of Christ and to know this love that surpasses knowledge that you may be filled to the measure of all the fullness of God. Bind wisdom around your head and neck and add discretion for leading a peaceable life, as well as, peace in your health [Proverbs 3:1-8]. The New Covenant releases the Lord glorious riches to loyal covenant believers. The Bible tells us in [Proverbs 1:5] A wise man will hear and will increase learning; and a man of understanding shall attain unto wise counsels.

A covenant relationship, like a marriage, is the eternal bond of peace formed by walking together in thought...like mindedness...on one accord...life agreement. The Bible tells us in [Amos 3:3] Can two walk together unless they agree. Transformation takes place through agreement...the Spirit...your mind, heart and actions. An ungodly yoke corrupts, pressures and weakens the mind, but the yoke of Christ is easy, full of grace, full of promises, authority, wisdom and strength [**Matthew 11:28:30**]. Jesus walks with us, talks to us, teaches us, corrects us and gives rest for our souls through the yoke of agreement initiated by His revelation. There is no failure, insecurities or uncertainties when the heart truly walks in agreement with Jesus. Who or what a soul is yoked or united with reveals who the soul is in agreement with. An ungodly yoke is defined as a heavy burden (bound around the neck) that brings the weaker one under subjection to its chain of command and trickery. Weights such as anxiousness, desperation, nervousness, frustrations, worries, difficulties, uncertainties, insecurities or failure can lead to sin and develop a yoke of bondage from not trusting GOD. Yokes and weights that are not meant for us to carry can be broken… crushed through a worship experience, a surrendering of it all. Pure worship… intimacy with the Lord… is a covenant blessing and power weapon for the Church that will destroy strongholds in the mind. This breaks that yoke off the neck. Think about this. The spine is connected to the base of the neck which permits movement of the body and mental connection. Unequally yoked gives the devil the opportunity to lead and control the body. This gives control into the head in order to bind one. Notice, the neck symbolize movement and direction of the head where dreams, vision, instruction, strategies and purpose are formed and attacks are aimed. The head spiritually speaking symbolizes influence, covering, direction, thinking, knowledge, power, focus and where salvation (the helmet) protects the persuasion of GOD in the mind [**Ephesians 6:17**]. As stated in the above paragraph, Proverbs caution us to bind wisdom as a garland around the neck never to let it leave or let it go.

The devil's plan is to strike through agreement causing immobility and to paralyze one from moving forward in their godly purpose or achievements as GOD desires for one by His way. **The Bible tells us in [2 Corinthians 6:14] Do not be unequally yoked; what fellowship can light have with darkness or what do righteousness**

have with wickedness? And what fellowship has light with darkness? The Church is commanded to stand firm and do not let yourself be trapped or burdened by the yoke of slavery/ bondage. The Bible speaks expressively on the consequences of being unequally yoked. This spiritual truth warns the Church not to form bonds, ties or close attachments with unbelievers. We may associate with people, but there should be a spiritual sensitivity like a radar that sends a signal in reference to whom you allow to bond with you and who you bond with. Unequally yoke can cause compromise, spiritual dullness to form, identity thief, the light to diminish and the oil to be removed as with the five foolish virgins. These are other forms of yokes which can be equal or unequal… grow in either direction such as: marriage yoke, job yoke, career yoke, finance yoke, emotional yoke and success yoke. *Unequally yoked comes from the Greek word heterozugeo which means bound, unevenly matched or holding different values that are contrary to faith.* This includes the deceit that can come through forms of rules, appearance and persuasion. **The Bible tells us in [John 3:36] Whoever believes in the Son has eternal life; whoever does not obey shall not see life, but the wrath of God remains on him.** The word believes here means a persuasion that arouses the heart to long term action with confidence: action of faith, action of love and action of obedience; experiencing a measure of the eternal blessings in this life. The way of the CROSS is ABBA holy counsel toward man's recovery, sanctification and how the very act of being forgiven erases the past with all traces of guilt, all traces of shame and coldness. The Power of the CROSS of Jesus elevates the heart, renews the mind and transforms the soul by the Holy Spirit. The Power of the CROSS washes the conscience guilt clear with righteousness (the blood, new garment) and makes us flawless in the eye of GOD… creating the upright flow through Christ. Remember, the message of the CROSS speaks freedom, covenant, baptism, nearness to GOD, identification, sacrifice, love, triumph and the wisdom of GOD.

There are blood pacts formed out of the spirit of fear, wrong perception, wrong influence, such as, transgenderality, homosexuality, gangs, lesbianism, wiccan, white power, black power, clan, adultery, sovereign citizen, idolaters, warlock, witch and secret organizations or secret society, etc. And there are blood pacts that many in the Church seem to fall prey to through the lack of knowledge, lack of commitment, a void in the soul, agreement, acceptance, motives, covet and wantonness. A blood pact is a demonic contract agreement signed with the life -blood- of a soul over to satan. The power influence behind such blood pacts is evil and wicked in source. Blood pacts can only be demolished by the Power of the CROSS of YESHUA… His Blood Potency and the soul's renunciation and surrendering agreement! The Lord Jesus Christ is the only source of power and fulfillment that can fill the void in any soul. A soul may not see it as a blood pact or turning their back to GOD due to spiritual blinders and denial or due to the control of the entity. The first wicked blood pact was developed through the fall in the Garden of Eden; the persuasion was spiritual and the manifestation was physical. Eve (Adam) sold their souls to the devil… made a pact with satan. Everything originates from a seed (good or evil) and a seed produces roots and trees. When the root of a thing is uprooted, then every thought, vision and creativity connected to that seed will be stopped… nullified. (Purchase Bloodline Spiritual DNA) When the root is discerned its' seed can be destroyed through the Power of the finished work of the CROSS through the Word. Blood pacts are not only physical, but spiritual because they are formed through demonic agreement. Blood pacts can be a threat to ones life or livelihood. They can be formed through ceremonial rituals, casual sex, oral sex, sexual gadgets, incest, porn, wild parties, hazing, masturbation, blindfolded acts, promises and oaths alliance sworn in alliance privately or openly before a whole group or organization. Some Fraternity and Sorority unknowingly or knowingly rejecting Truth and Light make pledges through rituals that are ungodly. One may not see it in that Light that's why we should search the scriptures in order to understand when and what was birthed by whom; and where did it come from, how and why. These blood pacts form ungodly soul ties and oaths that violate the Christian faith and deny the Power of the CROSS. No matter how one may justify its means or do charitable deeds or attend church the root of it is abominable, vile and offensive in the sight of GOD who is holy and just and full of wisdom. The performance of fraternity or sorority done in some churches in the sanctuary of GOD is unholy and abominable to Him. It's rooted in idolatry. This also applies to areas pertaining to the music industry. God's wisdom is the spiritual eye of discernment into the nature of a thing or situation. ABBA shares neither His throne nor temple (believers) with no idols. Remember, GOD loves the sinner, but GOD abhors the sin; therefore, the way of escape and hope is through the wisdom of Yahweh revealed in Christ. **The Bible tells us in [Joshua 24:14-15a] Now therefore fear the LORD and serve him in sincerity and in faithfulness. Put away the gods that your fathers served beyond the River and in Egypt and serve the LORD. And if it is evil in your eyes to serve, choose this day whom you will serve, whether the gods your fathers served in the region beyond the River or the gods of the Amorites in whose land you dwell.** A lot of the movements, chants, dancing and folklore of such originated from the fathers that rejected GOD and offered themselves as sacrifices unto their gods.

There are principles (pure or impure) through agreement that governs the spirit world **[Genesis 2:17]**. These laws when activated in the earth through agreement free satan to work or Holy Spirit to work… opens the door to wickedness or to goodness… good or evil. **The Bible tells us in [Matthew 4:4] Man Shall NOT live by bread alone, but by Every WORD that Proceeds from the Mouth of God.** God's Word! God's Promises! That's Reality. **The Bible tells us in [Proverbs 18:20-21] A man's belly shall be satisfied with** the fruit of his mouth; and with the increase of his lips shall he be filled. Death and life is in the power of the tongue and they that love it shall eat the fruit there of. For by thy WORDS thou shall be justified and by thy WORDS thou Shall be condemned. The adversary through the instrument of the serpent, as well as, Adam in the book of Genesis demonstrates how the law of speaking (words) and the law of agreement are powerful. **The Bible tells us in [Leviticus 5:4-6, 10] If a person swears, speaking thoughtfully with his lips to do evil or to do good, whatever it is that man may pronounce by an oath and it is hidden from him when he realizes it, then he shall be guilty in any of these matters. And it shall be when guilty in any of these matters that he shall confess that he has sinned in that thing...** The mouth and tongue members represent speech of words which is powerful. Words (vows-oaths) can lead to healthy journey or a breach (violation-gap) in the spirit. Our words are seed and that which is seed affects the supernatural and earthly sphere. Vows and promises of loyalty should only be reserved for God's way. We must be aware and cautious of what or who we connect ourselves to or with. Acts of omission and commission should be confessed to receive the grace that is already available through the Lamb of GOD. When an individual(s) is involved in practices that lead away from faith, affection and loyalty to GOD the sin must be confessed and all ties abandoned. BREAK The CHAIN! CUT THE CORD! If one rejects GOD by rejecting His Word, GOD will reject that soul also **[2 Kings 17:15; Isaiah 1:28; Matthew 10:33; John 12:48]. The Bible tells us in [Galatians 5:19-21] Now the practices of the sinful nature are clearly evident: Adultery, Fornication, Lasciviousness, Idolatry, Witchcraft, Hatred, Emulations, Wrath, Strife, Sedition, Variances, Heresies, Envying, Murder, Drunkenness, Revelling and such like; of which I tell you before, as I have also told you in time past, those that practice such things will not inherit the**

Kingdom of God. Take heed, the Bible warns the Church of the falling away (souls) that happens from within the body of Christ.

Remember, ungodly soul-ties are a result of reacting to wrong reasoning or wrong wisdom: the lust rooted in the heart that is conceive and gives birth to sin. Organizations that hold ceremonial rituals are usually held outside or enclosed in a dark room with candles, chanting, pledges, altar and tables; some contain diagrams on the floor with candles, tracing boards, all seeing eye, goats head, eastern star, skulls, animal sacrifice, crossbones aprons, coffins and kneeling at the altar are rooted in Luciferian doctrine; the doctrine of devils **[1 Kings 18:21; Deuteronomy 4:19; Ezekiel 8:16]**. This false worship petitions evil just as the ancestors' altars petitioned evil and wickedness. This was forbidden then and JESUS says it is still forbidden today. The day the soul eats of its fruit that soul shall surely die... such practices are forbidden. Death relates to spiritual blindness and spiritual deafness, fallen relationship, marred image and physical death. This altar with its practices is not the same as the altar of Jesus Christ! This is a form of Baal worship patterned after pagan worship... occultism... symbols that represent falsehood, satan, death, idol worship which opposes the finished work of the CROSS and open doors to spiritual blindness, self deceit and infirmities, Ancestor's altars (altars erected through rebellion and hard heartedness) due to its habitation and origin can release bondage, confusion, unbelief, compromise, restriction and infirmities of the mind and body through its demonic spiritual umbilical cord; which can manifest or pass through the bloodline or generations from a ungodly connection. Therefore, as Holy Spirit open eyes and ears, it's a great reward and relief to repent and renounce things that were apart of our ancestor's generation that can pass to another generation because of their hatred of GOD and evil practices. Although we may haven't had direct relationship, the Bible reveals clearly where things originated, their influence and what He say about it. **The Bible tells us in [Exodus 20:5-6] Thou shalt not bow down thyself to them, nor serve them; for the LORD thy God am a jealous God, visiting the iniquity of the fathers upon the children unto the third and fourth generation of those that hate me; And shewing mercy unto thousands of them that love me and keep my commandments.** Grace extends this provision through humility and obedience on our part, apart from pride and destruction. Baphomet god (half goat half human idol) falls under Baal religion and worship. We see this in many performers' videos today. They knowingly and openly show you what influences their wealth and fame regardless of who is infected with its toxin because of lustfulness and the lack of knowledge of the divine Truth of a matter. Just as gangs have signs and symbols so does ungodliness and idolatry. These symbols are birth under Baal worship and therefore are satanic in origin. The Bible refers to this has witchcraft! Jesus provides the ultimate solution to resisting the seductiveness of pagan idol worship. He demonstrated that He alone holds all power over demons, sending them to the Abyss **[Luke 8:31]**. He exalts us in due season as we humble and seek His face. He promises those who repent, love and trust in Him will overcome all evil and the forces of Hades (underworld) shall not overpower the believer in Christ **[Matthew 16:18]**. As a believer in Christ is given divine revelation and wisdom's discernment the Spirit of Life breathes, takes captive, dismantle the evil and the wisdom of GOD causes the soul to prevail.

YESHUA (Jesus) is the only Master to be served as Master. He is the property owner and spiritual head of the Church. The Church is governed only by ONE called ADONAI (Master) **[Matthew 9-10]**. Taking an oath or bowing to something else outside of the provisions of GOD in loyalty offends Him and gives that force power over its' subjects. This is called double mindedness and hypocrisy. Although the deed is natural, in the spirit realm it opens doors to other possible factors to build up resistance within a soul. The higher the rank one reach in a fraternity or Masonic the more of what was hidden and kept secret is exposed through the altar of ceremony ritual for blood (life)… with depraved promises of power linked to the yoke of pride and covetousness. Things which appear as innocence, rewarding, with approval and fun on the surface can have a hidden spiritual connection in the spirit world. We came from Elohim, who is Spirit. Spirit created male and female and Spirit breathed Spirit-Himself into us and made us a spirit-soul before the fall. This reveals that we are spiritual beings inside of a body **[Genesis 2:7]**. GOD breathed breathe-life into man and gave man His Spirit, His nature and His kingdom. The devil don't like or care for mankind; his mission attempt is to take to pieces your crown, ruin your character, disqualify you from the race, remove the believer out of divine position and mislead the soul for self destruction. **The Bible tells us in [Revelation 21:8] But the fearful and unbelieving and the abominable and murders and whoremongers and sorcerers and idolaters and all liars shall have their part in the lake which burneth with fire and brimstone: which is the second death.** This is revelation John revealed to the Church about the unbelieving. GOD does not share His children with no other gods. And His children aren't to share ourselves with another lover… false gods. A soul that's born of GOD Spirit bears the Name of the LORD… His Name! There is no level of ranking in loyalty to ONE. GOD is very clear on where He stands in His sovereignty as the one true GOD. He doesn't rank or compromise with idols over one's loyalty… the choice is left up to the individual to choose life or death, good or evil and pure or impure. *Loyalty is a strong faithfulness, a fullness of devotion or alliance and obedience to someone or something.* A spouse doesn't share there spouse with another lover for the sake of fun, gain, testing the waters, pay back or acceptance which is compromise. GOD is a jealousy GOD for His name sake. Therefore, Yahwism and Baalism did not co-exist in the Bible, nor can they co-exist together today. The Fire of the LORD devours Baal practices and all of its variation forms. If a soul finds oneself in idolatry which is spiritual adultery move swiftly to the place of acknowledgement and repentance and faithfulness to Jesus... no guilt recorded. Turn your back to blood guiltiness and shamefulness and your face and heart completely to Christ Jesus. Break the Chain!

Everything has an origin; just as the noose and the cross origin which still sounds off an alarm in the world today. Origins do not change, but the names of activities, groups, entertainment, practices or activations throughout generations do. That in it self exposes the demonic spiritual entry that opens the crossover into false worship and falsehood; although it has the look of innocence and share of good deeds... its origin is deception. The devil knows how to use his tool of falsehood; the root of him is cursed no matter what acts of charities he promotes through bamboozle. If the core of a thing is evil the whole thing is corrupt. JESUS is the Healer! **The Bible tells us in [Colossians 2:8] See to it that no one takes you captive through hollow and deceptive philosophy, which depends on human traditions and the elemental spiritual forces of this world rather than on Christ.** Just as a race and a culture have history and customs, the Church has history and heathen nations have history. And history good or bad, evil or good will pass on its tradition of influence. Researching and dissecting Biblical history about the origin and how it relates to the believer today rules out entrapment, enslavement and bondage. There is nothing new under the sun. The question we should ask ourselves is "What does The LORD say about it?" If GOD declares a thing unholy, then it's unholy. If GOD declares a thing detestable, then it's detestable. If GOD declares a thing blessed, then it is blessed. Many have witness on worldwide news colleges and families that have experienced extreme situations due to ritual activities in the name of fun and acceptance. Blood pacts (contracts, promises or agreements) must be renounced and denounced by individuals. The GRACE of GOD Is SUFFICIENT

AND HIS LOVE IS FOREVER ABOUNDING! Yeshua's love is not artificial or superficial or temporary; His love is endless action manifested through compassion and mercy.

Ex-souls of Freemasonry, Illuminati have testified openly (youtube) of their escape from darkness through Grace and Truth and have been set free by the Power of the CROSS of JESUS (Yeshua); now sharing their testimonies to help others see the LIGHT of Christ by exposing darkness and deception of organizations. **The Bible tells us in [Psalm 119:130] The entrance of thy words give light and understanding unto the inexperience.** JESUS is the Restorer of the soul! **The Bible tells us in [Deuteronomy 13:6-8] If any brother, the son of thy mother or thy son or daughter or the wife of thy bosom or your friend which is as thine own soul, entice thee secretly saying, "Let us go and serve other gods which you have not known, nor thy fathers; Namely of the gods of the people which are round about you, nigh unto you or far off from you, from the one end of the earth even unto the other end of the earth; Thou shalt not consent unto him nor hearken unto him, neither shall thine eye pity him, neither shalt thou spare, neither shalt thou conceal him...** The enemy behind the scene does not approach with open intent to harm, but with an underlined intent to grip, persuade through vain philosophy, vain fun, enticing words and bring mental and bodily enslavement. The devil plots through the form of deception and his desire is to desensitize increasingly throughout generations for the Antichrist agenda.

The spirit of compromise and seduction doesn't forbid a soul of their claims to Christ, but the pathway introduces the door for serving multiple gods (polytheistic religion) for sensual pleasures and material gain. Such doors will not reveal its deception. Wild parties, ceremony rituals, branding (tattooing), body piercing and sex rituals where worship acts performed by the foreign nations... those nations that where enemies of the LORD by choice... idolaters. If one falls back into the ways of the world such practices that aren't mentioned can also attract the soul to indulge in its habitation. This is the interaction of how false altars are established today. The power of GOD living in you is not to be denied or rejected… this is called having a form of godliness, but denying the power thereof **[2 Timothy 3:5-7]**. When Moses came down from receiving the Ten Commandments, the people had fallen into every vivid form of idolatry… spiritual adultery, due to their lack of trust, lack of the knowledge of GOD and carnal desires. This is how apostasy slowly shapes and reveals itself today. They made themselves a golden calf of gold with names of gods written upon it. They quickly reverted back to what they had been influenced by and exposed to during there time of oppression in slavery. Moses stood at the entrance of the camp and said whoever is for the LORD come to me and those that rebelled where slaughtered **[Exodus 32:19-30]**. JESUS is our Deliverer! **The Bible tells us in [Joshua 24:15]… but for me and my house, we will serve the LORD. If any man lack wisdom, let him ask of God, who gives to all liberally and without reproach and it will be given [James 1:5]. The fear of the LORD is the beginning of wisdom and knowledge of the Holy One is understanding [Proverbs 9:10].** Just as there is spiritual wisdom, knowledge and understanding, there is also worldly, demonic and man's wisdom, knowledge and understanding which are not the same in nature or spirit. The Babylonians and the Canaanites practiced body cutting and branding in showing homage and honor to their many gods… man and demonic wisdom combined. Entertaining unrestrained or unbridled carnality keeps a soul attached to the things of this world and spiritual senses dull. True Light attaches souls to the things of the true living GOD. The Light of TRUTH prepares us for the end times and the Wisdom of GOD keeps those that embrace it sound, strong and secure. **The Bible tells us in [Proverbs 2:6-7] For the LORD gives wisdom, from his mouth come knowledge and understanding, He holds success in store for the upright,**

He is a buckler to those who walk uprightly. The yoke of Christ snatches the soul from the love of this world and its elements of deception… angel worshipping, sun, moon and star worshipping… graven images… any other falsehood… the worshipping of what the Creator created instead of the Creator **[Exodus 20:4-6]**; all other unrepented sins that cause the soul to grow callous toward the Truth…the Power of the CROSS…BREAK The CHAIN! Eternal wisdom builds, teaches, perfects skillfulness, preserves, disciplines and governs the appetite and passions of those that ask for it… ask the LORD for wisdom increase.

As time pass from generation to generation satan's plan is to keep the soul distracted, misguided and deluded. As this increase, when the time comes for the mark of the beast initiation in the hand or forehead by the Antichrist, it may come with a lesser strain to take a mark or brand which will be the mark of the beast 666 in whatever form it appears to come. **The Bible tells us in [Revelation 13:16-18] And he causes all, both small and great, rich and poor, free and bond to receive a mark in their right hand or in their foreheads: And that no man might buy or sell, save he that had the mark or the name of the beast or the number of his name. This calls for wisdom. If anyone has insight… understanding let him calculate the number of the beast, for it is the number of man and his number is 666.** The mark will be as a seal of end-time identification for the followers of the Antichrist and his false prophet (spokesman) will cause people to take this mark. Taking the mark of the beast will indicate a turning from GOD to a governmental system that will control buying, selling and living or death for keeping alliance to GOD. And the other side in taking the mark of the beast will indicate eternal damnation… **[Amos 3:3]** the covenant of agreement transaction. We are in the end times… choose freedom… choose life… the Power of the finished work of the CROSS that speaks to the past, present and future. Remember, as the redeemed of the LORD our identification and newness of life is formed and from Him only. The Church is to identify ourselves with our Redeemer who lives… YESHUA HAMASHIACH THE SON OF THE LIVING GOD!

The altar is connected to the temple of GOD in the tabernacle. It is where the sacrifice of offering is laid prostate as a sweet fragrance and worship unto the LORD. This is important because this very act relates to the believer as a spiritual altar offering a sweet fragrance to GOD by the Fire of the Spirit. Our faculties, will, emotions and bodies are the altar of sacrifice that is to be consumed by the Fire of GOD. The Spirit of GOD adds His Holy Fire making us blameless before GOD, making us fit to come into His Presence, fit for kingdom purpose and fit to meet with Him as we prostrate our life as an offering unto Him. This is pure worship… intimacy that brings a life of kingdom dominance, transformation and deliverance. There were two altars in the tabernacle, the altar of burnt offerings (also called bronze, brazen or sacrifice) and the altar of incense. *Altar comes from the Hebrew word 1. mizbeach (Strong's Concordance) means a place of slaughter or sacrifice… giving up of oneself 2. Greek word thusiaterion (Strong's Concordance) meeting place between GOD… to draw near to GOD.* The place where the LORD meets, exchange and commune with the repentant called the worshiper. The altar of the LORD is not the same in any reflection to the ancestors' altars of Baal (which exists today in many forms). The CROSS is the altar revealing the message of Yahweh's favor of what it cost to be forgiven, cost to be healed, cost be reconciled, cost to be set free, cost to walk in freedom's liberty and cost to be hidden in Christ; what is now already done concerning the true and pure Church. That which GOD predetermined He provides and releases to a people through the message of the finished work of the CROSS at Calvary. Our greatest weapon in working out our own salvation in fear and trembling is to understand the revelation and activate the wisdom of the Power of the CROSS which destroys falsehood, the lies, the yoke of slavery and unleash with evidence the favor that stooped down in mercy to mankind; those are inferior to His supremacy [**John 3:16**]. That's Favor! The greatest suffering, the greatest love and the greatest victory took place at Calvary to revive and create the way for souls to come near and live in harmony with GOD. Many believe, but many fall short in faithfully trusting GOD. He wants your heart... a heart prostrate before Him. BREAK the CHAIN! LORD, I Release It All At The CROSS! **The Bible tells us in [Proverbs 3:5-6] Trust in the LORD with all your heart and lean not on your own understanding; in all your ways submit to him and he will make your paths straight.** This level of trust divinely shifts the atmosphere because it recognizes and causes the soul to bow to the sovereignty of All Mighty God. Trust causes us to step into a paradigm that is not comfortable to the flesh mindset. Trust at this level is the result of one's heart surrendering, the mind submitting, the casting off the cares, pains, weights and worries and conforming one's ways in humility in the face of temptation, disappointment, hurt, opposition or loss. It's a supernatural Holy Spirit confident impartation that's beyond human comprehending. This act of obedience "Trust in the LORD" releases the reality of GOD that is far beyond our intellect to perform in our affairs. Trust says trust GOD in all things at all times no matter what the outcome is. The CROSS is the measuring rod to use in what we engage, entertain, what engage us, what we say, how we live and how we act in secret, publicly and toward others. The CROSS of Love is our canopy for covenant blessings. The measuring rod corrects, rebukes and instructs when the heart is out of alignment with GOD. Soul! Soul! Come Into Holy Alignment In Jesus Name! This is the discernment and judgment call of eternal wisdom.

Apply the revelation and knowledge to the next spiritual level in governing your emotions, behavior and thought system today which flows from the heart. The Power of the CROSS is the grace and it is the same grace that frees any in prison in their mind. The believer's consciousness and behavior toward GOD, others and self is to reflect the freedom Christ provided on the CROSS because He lives within. This freedom is influenced and mastered only through the life of the Spirit working in the soul and the Power of the Blood spattered in the soul. The CROSS of Christ directs our future, purpose and accomplishments without limitations. Think about that! What held us as slaves before the CROSS experience is broken by the CROSS experience! Meditate on that! It is the Power of the finished work of the CROSS of Jesus that sustains a faithful people; a people that exercise faith and put faith to work. This divine restoration will demand the commitment of a continuous renewing of the mind and heart. Every life issue that we face, hidden, swept under the rug or not to be talked about will call forth this grace of glory dimension to be set in motion. Whatever you have been told not to tell or keep it to your self is a trick from the devil; take it to the CROSS where there is room for favor and healing. The CROSS deals with every dark place of the past, religious spirits, traditions apart from the will of GOD and your assignment pertaining to His divine will. This eternal knowledge and authority confronts matters with justice, hope and healing. It is the prescription of wisdom's equity pertaining to the new life in Christ.

PERSONAL NOTES

Salvation is of the Lord

Father GOD, In the Name of Jesus, I give you my life and submit my soul to you. I turn from my idols or my self. I renounce them. I repent and receive your grace by faith. I believe in my heart Jesus Christ is the Son of God raised from the dead (to save my soul or forgive a backslider like me). I believe by faith unto righteousness and with my mouth I confess Jesus Christ as my Savior and my Lord. Jesus come into my heart that I may receive Eternal Life and live to live again. Fill me with your Holy Spirit and baptize me with the fire of Holy Spirit in Jesus Name. Amen.

> Romans 10:9-10
> Ephesians 2:8-9
> John 5:24
> Acts 2:38

---

* Water baptism is the outer expression, testimony, act of obedience and spiritual identification of Christ circumcising our hearts, submerged into His death (old man) and resurrected (new man) into the Kingdom of God by His Spirit.

What greater love has no man than this to lay down His life for His friends; friends that He calls friend, no longer a slave or a servant, through His blood and by His Spirit regardless of mistakes, embarrassments and shame, because He heals them. Friends whom He makes known the mystery of His Father's Kingdom… secrets and revelations hidden from the world **[John 15:13-15]**. Yet, the LORD delights through acceptance to apply His blood to keep his friends in the place of divine protection, divine peace and clothed in righteousness, bright and spotless. The blood-spattered CROSS removes frequencies of defense, fears, fortresses, hesitations and constraints out of the soul and the way of thinking. The Power of the CROSS is the plumb line that distinguishes; separates trust from fear, justice from injustice, holy from unholy, angelic from demonic and clean from unclean **[Isaiah 28:16-17]**. Being set free is broad and intense in the grace of Yahweh. For example: when a person's body undergoes a major surgery the whole body responds to the pain and the healing that gradually happens inwardly. And when a major surgery is needed, but rejected that cause's internal, as well as, external damage. Likewise, when the Favor of GOD, His righteousness in Christ, is imputed to the heart, the Holy Spirit infusion in the soul causes the soul to experience a supernatural divine change from within that reflects in the condition of one's heart, mind, soul, body and life extended term. The favor of GOD infused by the Holy Spirit also causes the soul to shine in Truth and walk in kingdom purpose. Only that which is upheld by the favor of GOD has eternal fiber that nurtures from the inside. This eternal supernatural holy fiber causes your behavior, conversation to response to the inner work. The Blood and the Spirit does a supernatural surgery in the heart, mind and soul to deliver a fruitful increase.

ABBA's FAVOR

- **The Favor of GOD Guards His Presence**

- **The Favor of GOD Clears, Opens and Directs Paths**

- **The Favor of GOD is Evidence of His Holy Justice and Inheritance**

- **The Favor of GOD is Evidence of His Divine Approval and Acceptance**

- **The Favor of GOD does NOT Exempt the Believer from Unfavorable Circumstances**

- **The Favor of GOD Sustains and Empowers the Believer To Activate the Kingdom of GOD from that Place**

- **The Favor of GOD Rests Upon Trustworthy, Loyal and Submissive Hearts with Promotion**

- **The Favor of GOD Draws the Presence of The LORD**

- **The Favor of GOD Is God's Favor NOT Man's**

The finished work of the CROSS of JESUS benefits the totality of believers in Christ as strangers in this foreign land. The Church understands the foundation that the Savior who was sent as a drink offering, peace offering and guilt offering was crucified for the sins of the world; bleed, forgave, died and was resurrected to give the gift of everlasting life and ascended to send the comforter. The first saying Christ uttered on the CROSS was "Father Forgive Them They Know Not What They Do" and the sixth utterance was "It Is Finished" [Luke 23:34]. These are two of the most powerful demonstrative words of encouragement and victory flow for the advancement of the Church. This flow is God's supernatural giving the Church, believers, His ability upon our powerlessness to engage as He did by the Holy Spirit. This greatness demonstrates the way to a life of holiness, a life of assurance, compassion and mercy, productivity, wholesomeness, agreement, steadfastness, warfare, longsuffering, peace and favor [John 3:16-21; Romans 5:1; 6:22]. Think about what it cost and what that cost included! It's there at the CROSS Jesus abolished hostility and where the veil was torn that separated Yahweh and man which signified the "ONLY" way to GOD. Without the blood of Christ the way to GOD the Father is closed off to mankind due to fallen nature (revolt). The thick veil was a foreshadow of the Son of GOD flogged, bruised, bloody and lacerated body as a ransom for sinners. The torn veil symbolized Jesus Christ body that suffered death on the CROSS and conquered death sting (the grave) to reconcile sinners back to GOD [2 Corinthians 5:19]. Christ removed the separation that blocked the way from coming into loving fellowship with GOD and from entering into His holy Presence. The reality is found in Christ alone; the King of Glory! It's there at the CROSS Jesus conquered the force of evil and shows the believer in Christ the way of triumph. Evil force is what the enemy uses against us to weigh our minds down with matters we cannot change in our own ability. That force of weight can turn into a struggle in the soul which is ordained to be dealt in the power reality of the CROSS. In death on the CROSS JESUS disarmed those evil powers working against us **[Colossians 2:15]**; delivering all who will believe and trust Him from the Kingdom of darkness through His resurrection. The work of the CROSS released the Eternal World Order for freedom in Christ and righteousness to live life through the Power of the Spirit and to do the Fathers' business. This is the same power that raised JESUS from the dead. As a result, the believer's liberty in Christ Jesus is provided with God's power *(Greek word for power kratos meaning supernatural God power, demonstrative, eruptive, outward visibility and tangible)* in the earth realm that transcends the sphere and power of darkness, environments, locations, dimensions and time. Remember, this wisdom is understanding **[Proverbs 8:14]** and getting understanding develops a GOD conscience. If the LORD hates evil and wickedness **[Proverbs 8:13]**, we should hate it; yet, GOD principles will cause the writing on the wall to appear... don't compromise... be strong in the LORD and in the power of His might **[Ephesians 6:10]**. When there is understanding and acceptance of that knowledge, action is put forth and changes occur. The law of sin and death which cause guilt and shame was nailed to the CROSS along with every other hell hound that stands presently in the way of GOD and sincere hearts. The adversary may roar like a lion, but he has no power over those hidden in Christ who understands their legal rights in the Kingdom of GOD. The devil prowls, looking for an entry into the soul in order to devour **[1 Peter 5:8]**. *The word devour in the Greek means to squander, eat at until it is no more... destroy little by little.* The Church is supernaturally authorized to resist the devil, withstand any attack, be sober, watchful and to stand firm in the faith... Christ Died... Christ Crucified... Christ Resurrected... Christ Glorified... Christ seated at the right hand of authority of the Father. Therefore, believers are to anticipant with expectation the same mighty power of GOD which raised Yeshua from the dead has raised every believer and also given us the ability to operate by and in His Spirit.

One downfall that can separate a soul from GOD for all eternity is its unbelief; as the thief that hung at Calvary beside the Messiah denying Him to the point of death. Unbelief opens the door to spiritual poverty, spiritual death and alienation with GOD which leads to eternal condemnation. The spirit of condemnation will bow guard a soul from walking in the Truth due to the souls incompetence and unworthiness of its past. Spirit of condemnation locks a mind to its past. A soul may realize Truth; yet, refuse or have no power to walk in it. The spirit of condemnation keeps one walking and attached to the past. The spirit of condemnation keeps the soul black... some have been called the black sheep. This is the work of condemnation holding a soul hostage in guilt, fear and pride and such barriers of shame, pinned in anger and rejection. The spirit of condemnation lies to the soul to keep it from progressing in the Light. Grace and mercy dimension is the opposite of and above the dimension of guilt and shame. Guilt and shame are rooted in condemnation. Disgrace and embarrassment are fruit of guilt. Guilt is the condition of wrong behavior not confessed or forsaken; spirit of shame will set in to close-in a soul and make one feel insecure, but secure in hiding. The Bible calls this a stronghold. Grace gives (eternal) life and condemnation gives (eternal) death which can be experienced in this life in measure. Grace speaks hope and condemnation speaks hopelessness. Grace releases act of kindness and good will toward others. Condemnation causes a breach to linger. Just as I've mentioned how grace works in stages, condemnation also works in stages to conquer a soul through the seed of guilt. The Power of the CROSS kills all of its root system and seed and set ablaze its' tentacles holding the soul captive. This calls for deliverance and repentance. **The Bible tells us in [Isaiah 53:12] Therefore will I divide him a portion with the great, and he shall divide the spoil with the strong; because he hath poured out his soul unto death: and he was numbered with the transgressors; and he bare the sin of many, and made intercession for the transgressors.**

The believer's prosperity is complete; indulge in the Word of GOD, partake in intercession with faith and obedience. **The Bible tells us in [1 Samuel 15:22] To obey is better than sacrifice.** The one grace that unifies a soul to GOD for all eternity is its persistent faith in Christ; as the other thief that hung at Calvary willingly received the LORD to the point of life after death. Faith unlocks the door continuously to spiritual prosperity, answered prayers, victory in life, purpose and eternal life... experiencing a measure of heaven's covenant blessings on this side. Energetic faith is the provision (eye) of GOD leading His people and releasing the impossibilities from the eternal realm into the natural realm... grace extends beyond boundaries. Understanding the Power of the CROSS Yeshua (Jesus) endured supernaturally advances those that believe and trust with the ability to function under pressure and in creative purpose in times of transitioning forward from one level to the next level and so on; even from the bottom to the top. Remember, GOD promotes through His work of grace.

Just as the CROSS of Yeshua HaMashiach (Jesus Christ) is looked upon by many as being hideous, breathe taking, life taking, undesirable, disturbing, dreadful and too awful to be expressed by words is also the description of how transgression and iniquity are looked upon by God's justice and holiness as hideous, detestable, condemnable, unpardonable, unjustifiable, life taking and unthinkable. It is the Power of the CROSS and the Power of the Spirit that makes heaven's reality a reality in the earth realm for a believing soul. It is the Blood of JESUS applied to the heart that satisfies the LORD holy justice toward us. This is the believer's in Christ power and authority. Where the blood is applied in faith to the soul extraordinary changes occur, because the life in the blood ascends and goes beyond flesh limits. No case submitted is too hard or hopeless for the Power of the finished work of the CROSS. We do not fully know our own heart, but GOD is familiar with the intention and thought of it before salvation and since salvation; and has made the way of escape and healing relevant. **The Bible tells us in [Jeremiah 17:9-10] The heart is deceitful above all things and desperately wicked. Who can know it? I the LORD search the heart and examine the mind, to reward each according to their conduct.** This verse confirms that every soul will receive their due reward or judgment according to their conduct which means manner of life, deeds or ways. The heart operating in a fallen condition is corrupt and false just as the fallen seed that created the deed. It is man's carnal nature that blinds him and the lack of trust that brings deceit and shame. The heart is the object for continuous grace surgery through the Power of the CROSS and the Power of the Holy Spirit. The heart has to be placed on the altar of the Fire of the LORD that He may test and try to confirm its condition. The heart wickedness, deceitfulness and rebellion is as witchcraft **[1 Samuel 15:23; 1 John 3:4]**. GOD rewards the obedient with blessings and disobedient with curses. Obedience releases GOD divine favor, intervention and perfection will concerning the believer in Christ. Disobedience causes GOD to withhold His covenant blessings and to shut the heaven to errant souls. Its' deposit will blind hearts from Truth, will cause a soul to walk in deception, block deliverance, block healing, block mind-heart change, promote stubbornness, withdrawal, delayed obedience and promote rejection of Truth. REPENT! **The Bible tells us in [James 1:13-17] When tempted, no one should say, God is tempting me. For God cannot be tempted by evil, nor does he tempt anyone; but each person is tempted when they are dragged away by their own evil desire and enticed. Then, after desire has conceived, it gives birth to sin and sin when it is full grown gives birth to death. Don't be deceived, my dear brothers and sisters.** Forgiven grace eliminates this disease and sickness, but bondage eliminates freedom reality which brings on a backslidden action. The heart is a spiritual matter and the mind like the soul is a spiritual matter. GOD does not send temptation or tempts. It comes from the darkness that lies within the soul. The Power of the CROSS executes all confusion, rebellion, excuses, torment, double standards and mind games through peace with GOD. The cost at the CROSS gives abundant grace. And the soul must remain in fellowship with Jesus to experience His peace.

No human being is capable, fit or qualified to pay such a holy, eternal cost. Ask Holy Spirit to reveal to you of any unknown and known sins that can cause blockage. Examination is good for the soul…by the WORD. The Power of the CROSS is the answer for the soul and the answer for continuous freedom and victory. **The Bible tells us in [Romans 6:22-23] But now that you have been set free from sin and have become servants to God, the benefit you reap leads to holiness and the result is eternal life. For the wages of sin is death, but the gift of God is eternal life in Christ Jesus.** The Power of Christ that sets the soul free imparts His Spirit into the soul which is neither of this world nor does it have the mind faculty of this physical material world. This reflects the soul new life source and transition. This transition thrives, breathes and feeds (supernaturally) from the Holy Spirit like a baby connected to the umbilical cord in the womb. Disconnection causes a lack of oxygen which leads to separation and death. Bondage is similar to not having oxygen… a long term struggle… like compression on the chest cavity… restriction of life. Spiritual bondage is the source of physical bondage. It may appear from the outside arousing a step back from you. The spirit of bondage functions through the mind is to stagnate or detour one's development and to cause fatal issues by targeting one's mind for domination and to bring it into imprisonment.

The Spirit of the LORD is the required oxygen for freedom over all battles which start in thought, imagination… soulish. When the mind-spirit is healed the soul is healed and this strength comes through the inborn nature of GOD. **The Bible tells us in [Proverbs**

18:14] The spirit of a man will sustain his infirmity. The Bible tells us in [John 5:4] For whatever is born of God overcomes the universe. This is the victory that has overcome the world; our faith. This verse didn't say if, but whatever is born of GOD overcomes the universe. See it through the mind-Spirit of Christ: whatever is born or birth of the supernatural -GOD-overcomes... OVERCOMES the universe. That's deep revelation and truth. The GOD in us is greater. He lifts His standards above the universe and increases newness of minds from faith to faith, glory to glory. Such equity relates to the Power of the CROSS; eternally and internally. The Power of the CROSS holds divine influence ordained before the foundations of the world for the purpose predestined in GOD the Father for such a time as today in every phase in Church (believers in Christ) life and character. The Word of GOD is life to those who trust. JESUS breaks the chain, sets us free from spiritual poverty, bring believers into sonship, calls us friend, cloth us with the garment of righteousness, gives us a garment of praise for heaviness, gives us a new name, gives us His name and gives His Holy Spirit to teach us the walk of servanthood through sonship. Servanthood removes the "I" (ego) and replaces it with Jesus. Servanthood is not a slavery mentality, but it is the love of GOD in the heart working toward a common purpose for the greater good of the whole as friends of GOD. This guides us into the fulfillment of a practical life of harmony and devotion that the Church will live and experience the Kingdom of GOD in earth as it is in heaven.

It's the hideous, dreadful and horrific CROSS that displays the love of GOD for us today and forever more. It's this act of a love that is unconditional and grace that is amazing that brought about Jehovah (Yahweh) Judicial Justification, Restoration, Dominance, Advocacy, Righteousness, Purpose, Vision, Glory and Promise all summed up in the way of the bloody CROSS into full manifestation for hearts that will receive **[Romans 3:24-26]**. God's judgment demands that He judge sin and for this reason Yahweh's wrath will be upon all wicked and unrepentant souls. **The Bible tells us in [Colossians 3:5-6] Mortify therefore your members which are upon the earth; fornication, uncleanness, inordinate affection, evil concupiscence and covetousness, which is idolatry: for which things sake the wrath of God comes upon the children of disobedience. Ephesians 5:6… Let know man deceive you with empty words, for because of these things the wrath of God comes upon the sons of disobedience. Revelation 1:18… For the wrath of God is revealed from heaven against all ungodliness and unrighteousness of men, who by their unrighteousness suppress the truth.** Sin cannot exist in His Presence and bondage is arrested, stripped of its power in His Presence; prohibited to continue to harass and act. The life hidden in Christ is commanded to put to death such members that rise and were tolerated under the old nature through a deceitful and wicked heart. Such members cause division and strife in the union with GOD and should be put to death. Sin imprisons the soul, robs and destroys true identity, locks up the mind and the emotions and brings hostility against GOD and between the Soul and the Spirit.

Sin is a power that masters its subjects; no matter what the race or custom may be. Sin is not racist nor is it bound by shades of color or rank. **Apostle Paul tells us in [Romans 6:13-14] Do not go on offering members of your body to sin as instruments of wickedness. But offer yourselves to God as those alive raised from the dead (to new life) and your members as instruments of righteousness to God. For sin will no longer be a master over you, since you are not under the Law (as slaves), but under grace (favor and mercy).** We are reminded in both verses above that favor enables the believer to succeed over whatever may seem to be a struggle or challenge. Since the believer's life is Christ, that is the dimension authorized by Holy Spirit to shift the believer to another dimension to terminate sins' persuasion making one's conviction effective; throwing into panic sins' persuasion that comes to imprison the mind, as well as, the emotions. The body with its members is the source the other members work through **[Colossians 3:5-6]**; the abilities of the mind, emotions, will and body are to be sanctified, set apart, as instruments of righteousness through the Power of the CROSS. The Spirit of the LORD revealed the heart, mind and emotions (feelings) are the breathing grounds that receive good or evil, as well as, the grounds to create good or evil. This is where the choice of life and death are sown from. Keep in mind, the adversary wears a fine distinctive, clever disguise all so well in its craftiness and subtlety that can only be detected, spiritually discern or judged and overcome through the Power of the Holy Spirit. GOD has already designed the course for total freedom manifestation against conflict. The soul in Christ must eat from His vine **[John 15:3-7]**. The question is: Are you in love with Christ because He's certainly in love with you? Or are you in love with another lover… a counterfeit of the real deal… a perpetrator? Is He only Savior or both Savior and Lord? These are self examination questions to examine the man in the mirror. He wants to be LORD over your life; in every subject and chapter of it. This will stir up spiritual awareness, genuine love for GOD, spiritual gifts, knowledge and sound judgment.

Holy Spirit unfolded a divine moral rule which relates to the earthly and the spiritual. The word slavery, slave and servant are in the bible numerous times. Many today are offended by this word Cross, as well as, the Cross displayed inside the Church, but Holy Spirit deletes misunderstanding and confusion… yoke of bondage. As you study your Bible spiritual slavery and oppression are related throughout the history of the Church starting in the Old Testament which was not the Will of the Father, but generated through the seed of unbelief and disobedience (fallen nature) which brought about the curse of sin and death to all mankind and opened the pathway for such acts;

mankind having a love for darkness rather than light. The finished work of the CROSS is the answer to the depths, height, width and breadth of such decay and corruption... the Blood of JESUS... one righteous holy seed. It's vital to see enslavement with the revelation of GOD to recognize and receive divine Truth impartation. Holy Spirit desires the heart to understand how bondage and sin's control (wickedness, evil and perverseness) is paralleled to slavery and its control. GOD often uses visions, images, people and history as lessons, types and foreshadows to reveal the extremity of a divine spiritual Truth in order for the Church to know how to walk in Truth in this earthly sphere as friends of GOD. The common factors of forgiven and freedom is eternal love, wisdom and justice. As believers grow to understand and recognize the harm, meanness, calamity and degrading of a thing that the response should be to dismiss it altogether; give it no room to gain a foothold or grow. The common factors of sin and slavery equates ignorance... self centeredness... imprisonment... hostility... hatred... loss of covering... loss of estate and all that is not associated with being free. This is how GOD sees sin and what sinfulness does to the soul and heart that participate. The Power of the CROSS renders all pertaining to defeat and death powerless over souls that are in agreement with the complete work of the CROSS. Agreement which states one is actively in union. A free soul embraces its freedom continuous and the legal right to be free. Such souls don't look back or turn back to there bondage or what once enslaved them or that master. Souls that understand the sufficiency in the Power of the Blood and the CROSS will take hold of Truth and rise up in grace power that gave the soul freedom to break free of the chains that desire to hold the minds and emotions captive... through the Power of the Blood and the Holy Spirit, I command you to take into captivity all that seek to bind you. The Blood of JESUS annuls it and infuse supernatural peace within your heart. It's by faith.

PRAYER DECLARATIONS:

TAKE AUTHORITY BY THE POWER OF THE HOLY SPIRIT, BIND THE SPIRIT OF OFFENSE, HATRED, RAGE, REJECTION, LOW SELF ESTEEM AND ALL ITS KINDRED SPIRITS OF THE PAST THAT DICTATES TO YOU, COMMAND THEM NOW TO BE UPROOTED IN JESUS NAME! COMMAND THEM TO GO IN JESUS NAME! I DECREE WHOLENESS, THE PEACE OF GOD, VITALITY AND LOVE TODAY! TODAY IN MY SOUL, MIND, HEART AND BODY! SELF BE WHOLE IN JESUS NAME!

ALL THAT IS LEECHED TO YOUR SOUL TO SUCK LIFE OR SENT TO BRING HARM, SET YOU BACK OR DESTROY YOU, I DECREE ACCESS SHUTDOWN IN JESUS NAME! I TAKE HOLY GHOST AUTHORITY AND COMMAND UNCLEAN SPIRITS, FAMILIAR SPIRITS; MIND ALTERING SPIRITS, DESTINY THIEVES, HEXS, WITCHCRAFT PRAYERS, THREATS, MANIPULATION, ALL ACTS OF EVIL, WICKEDNESS AND SNARES TO BE DETHRONED! THROWN INTO ARRAY BY THE CONSUMING FIRE OF GOD! I TAKE AUTHORITY AND COMMAND BLESSING BLOCKERS TO BE THROWN INTO THE SEA, SPIRITUAL BLINDERS TO MELT, SPIRITUAL EYES SEE, SPIRITUAL EARS HEAR TODAY!!! SUFFICIENCY BE MULTIPLIED AND MANIFESTED THIS HOUR IN YESHUA'S (JESUS) NAME! I TAKE AUTHORITY AGAINST EVERY PERPETRATING SPIRIT AND THE PERPETRATOR'S PLAN, PLOT, ASSIGNMENTS AND COMMAND THEM TO MISCARRY IN JESUS NAME!!!

The Power of the CROSS of Christ releases a peace offering that no man can mentally comprehend. Peace with GOD gives the Church the legal right to encounter the Peace of GOD on all grounds from the death of love ones to the adversities in life. Peace with GOD is life in Christ and life that responds to Christ... the exceptional life of worthiness. Peace with GOD keeps and preserves believers in Christ from condemnation. The Peace of GOD extends far beyond what the natural man thoughts of peace comprehends as peace. Peace of GOD is His righteousness in our hearts that is demonstrated in our spiritual development and experienced in prayer to the LORD. Prayer releases the Lord's mind of peace. The divine Peace of GOD which is turned from vengeance is the opposite of His wrath (righteous indignation). Without Peace with GOD there is NO relationship to experience the Peace of GOD, neither His holiness nor promises. There is no partiality in the LORD. You may not understand it all, but the attributes which are Yahweh's nature comes through Christ and the work of the Holy Spirit into the soul. Christ is the Church peace advocate. The Peace of GOD is His fragrance of compassion, holiness, government, jealousy, protection, love and strength shielding like a blazing fire that stands unyielding in the heaven and as a light of glory for guiding all who belongs to Him through covenant kinship by way of the Blood of Jesus. The very Peace of GOD protects us from that which desires to harm us. Just because things happen or show up does not mean it has a legal right to prosper. Something that seems so innocent can be so wrong. Think about that! Measure it by the plumb line of GOD. **The Bible tells us in [Isaiah 54:17] No weapon that is formed against thee shall prosper and every tongue that shall rise against you in judgment thou shall condemn. This is the inheritance of the servants of the LORD, and their righteousness is of me saith the LORD.** The end of this verse tells the Church why... His constitution never changes or fails His redeemed people. The LORD establishes all that He promises through divine peace. *Peace comes* *from the Hebrew word Shalom meaning harmony, wholeness, welfare, prosperity, tranquility and completeness.*

The Lord's peace, power, holiness and righteousness guard against all that opposes the royal priesthood of GOD. Remember, though it comes it shall not prosper as the Church acknowledge GOD in all our ways and lean not to our own understanding. Yahweh's divine providence guards against the impurity of hearts and motives. It guards against false worship, the forces of evil, wickedness, temptation and condemnation. Divine peace guards against satan's fiery darts, chain of command, trackers, monitors and influence that target believing trusting souls. In other words, the Peace of GOD may be experienced in faith by a trusting believer during troublesome times. The Peace of GOD is a shield of defense for the believer in Christ Jesus. All that opposes His holiness, favor and peace is left outside of the camp; not able to draw near His Presence... face to face. Peace with GOD is His justification of making one right with Him; His justice includes His complete nature. And all who are in covenant relation with Christ bearing His name, holiness and righteousness are as living sanctuaries prepared for covenant blessings. That's the Peace of GOD, the Holiness of GOD and the Righteousness of GOD with manifested benefits for believers provided through the Blood of Yeshua (Jesus). As believers wear this privileged cloak in the heart although it will attract friction, we must remind ourselves that we are sealed with the Promise that is an active supernatural power and that we're covered in the Blood of JESUS. That Promise is the Holy Spirit, the governing authority of the Kingdom of GOD in the earth sphere and heavenly sphere. He's like the umbilical cord feeds the Church supernatural life substance for life. It is the Peace of GOD that surpasses all understanding **[Philippians 4:7]** that we want to experience. GOD is Jehovah (Yahweh) Shalom; the GOD of Peace. **The Bible tells us in [Colossians 3:15] And let the peace of God rule in your hearts to which also you are called in one**

body and be ye thankful. God's peace is a gift from Him through blood kindred to experience beyond the exaggerated and temporary peace of this world. The Peace of GOD promotes an inner calmness and flows to the deepest valley and the highest mountain through having Peace with GOD by the Blood of Christ. The Peace of GOD is to rule in our hearts by surrendering to the influence of Holy Spirit which is sown and reaped through the favor of GOD. **The Bible tells us in [Galatians 5:22] But the fruit of the Spirit is love, joy, peace, long suffering, patience, kindness, goodness, faithfulness, gentleness and self control.**

In view of the fact that GOD is creator and the source of life, the atonement by His sacrifice was required for justification and to obtain peace with the Father on behalf of mankind sinfulness. We understand this far that the peace of Christ purchased our peace with His righteousness; His life. The rituals in Leviticus points to particular patterns of symbolism, types and foreshadows of JESUS, our LORD and SAVIOR, who was slain to take away the sins of the world fulfilled in His body for those who accept him and persevere in faith. Sin is extremely serious to GOD and payment for sin is costly. We need to be reminded of this… sin is eternally deadly and hell is hot. This is crucial in understanding why blood was needed as a payment for cleansing the conscience of blemishes and receiving the crown of eternal life victory. **The Bible tells us in [Leviticus 17:11] For the life of the flesh is in the blood; and I have given it to you upon the altar to make atonement for your souls.** The blood contained life and the life in the blood was the substitute presented to GOD for redemption for fallen nature. The earthly mind cannot comprehend the cost to be forgiven; you must recall scripture which is spiritual and natural when dealing with a spiritual problem residing through carnal nature… without shedding of blood there is no remission **[Hebrew 9:22]**; a spiritual problem with only one resolution.

GOD is Spirit; His Spirit births new spiritual life and the Blood of Christ is the covenant carrier of this perfect life. The high priest was instructed by Yahweh to enter to the Holy of Holies once a year to make an Atonement sacrifice on the Day of Atonement called Yom Kippur for fasting, repentance confession, forgiveness, cleansing and sanctification [**Leviticus 16:29-30, 23:27-28**]. The high priest presented GOD to the people and the people to GOD. He had to make a blood sacrifice first for his household, himself and the community. If the high priest was not right with GOD he would fall dead in the Holy of Holies [**Leviticus 16:2-4**]... God's Presence. No unauthorized fire could be placed on the altar. The altar and how it was handled was very sacred. The continual fire at the altar that never burn out is a picture of Christ presenting Himself on the believers' behalf [**Leviticus 6:12-13**]... His Spirit and Presence. The sin-trespass and guilt-offering was offered on the altar of fire in the outer court for wrongdoing, misbehavior, offense, misdemeanor, lapse, wickedness, evil, injustice, crimes, sin and the blood was splattered on the tent of meeting, in the Holy Place, on the altar and in the Most Holy Place [**Leviticus 16:11-19**]. The blood offering substitute represented remission for all sins and was consumed by fire. This is important because it is the Fire of GOD which expels, executes for the cleansing in our hearts and minds and makes known God's acceptance, guidance and communication to His children. Jesus is the peace offering on the altar of burnt offering which supplies all the covenant blessings of salvation that spring forth from the finished work of the CROSS. His glory is not shared with idols. GOD does not justify, tolerate or wink at sin. **The Bible tells us in [Acts 17:30] In the past God overlooked such ignorance, but now he commands all people everywhere to repent.** It is His Spirit might *kratos* to empower the heart, soul and mind with the power *endunamao* of GOD from within to withstand attacks against the soul and promote the new appetite for eternal blessings through the Blood of Yeshua (Jesus) [**Ephesians 1:19-20; 6:10**].

GOD required pure blood to be sprinkled on everything in the tabernacle (tent of meeting) and obedience from the people in order to obtain divine cleansing for the soul. The high priest applied blood to the atonement cover which is called the mercy seat in the Most Holy Place (Holy of Holies) where the Shekinah Glory of GOD, Yahweh's Presence, dwelled between the seraphim. The seraph, angels of highest order, positioned on top of the mercy seat symbolizes the reverence and safeguard of the Lord's Holiness and Glory Presence. The mercy seat is the Throne of GOD. The Throne of God is His Court of Constitutional Supreme Justice. All appeals, pleas, petitions, intercession, supplications, calls, songs, declarations, decrees, commands, crowns, mantles, gifts and covenant blessings are granted through the Blood of Jesus (Yeshua) directed to all that pertains to the Bride of Christ birthright and sonship whom He is head authority. The fragrance of a pure, unblemished sacrifice satisfied the courts of judgment for sin. The blood sprinkled on the atonement cover was the ransom for all repentant souls that year up until the next year. Where His pure blood (JESUS) is His Presence remains. In **Leviticus 16:9-10** two male goats where used for atonement by the high priest; the first goat, a substitute and sin offering sacrifice slain for the payment of the sins of the nation. The second goat called the Azazel known as the scapegoat, the high priest was to lay his hands on the head of that goat for the confessing of sins which was the transferring and removing of the nation of Israel's sin and guilt; then, sending away the scapegoat bearing all sin into the wilderness never to return. All of theses Old Testament temporary rituals had to be repeated yearly for the penalty of sin and covering over sin; in order for GOD of Covenant to sanctify and His Presence to dwell with the people. The sacrificial animal rituals did not have any authority, influence or power to cancel out, wash away or take sin out of the heart.

Learn by heart, only the Blood of JESUS brings God's cleanliness, sanctification and turns away His wrath. The New Covenant washes our sins away. **The Bible tells us in [Hebrew 4:15] For we do not have a High priest who is unable to emphasize with our weaknesses, but we have one who has been tempted in every way just as we are; yet did not sin.** GOD has supplied the Church with every spiritual blessing needed to maintain right fellowship with Him, be victorious and to ascend in prayer and supplication. Spiritual blessings such as: 1) chosen by Him before the foundation of the world 2) He makes us holy and blameless 3) offers salvation 4) gives power to become sons of God 5) receive full access to the Father 6) favorable in Christ through the blood 7) redeemed us from eternal condemnation 8) sanction to glorify God in our body and soul 9) debt cancellation 10) seated in heavenly places in Christ 11) gives the Church wisdom through His Word 12) we are part of His perfect plan through holy alignment 13) baptized in the Power and Fire of GOD Holy Spirit. As you study your Bible the inheritance goes on and on for the redeemed of the LORD. There is nothing left unturned or undone that the Blood and the Spirit did not cover. No excuses at the Gate of Heaven will be accepted. What faces the Body of Christ must be introduced to the Power of GOD today. All that comes to steer or move you and take your crown that GOD already has for you is overcome by the blood and the magnitude of His Word that is to be hidden in your heart during all seasons and afflictions. Deep calling unto the deep; continue to seek and pray to GOD that Holy Spirit will teach and reveal to you in your encounter experiences the power that GOD ordained and how to demonstrate that knowledge in faith and wisdom. Jesus Christ, the Church of GOD High Priest, has co-signed with each believer to intertwine them with His perfection at all times and in all matters. And by covenant agreement we are co-labors with the LORD. This power of agreement brings us into a state of maturity.

No man can sing their own praises of what the Spirit of GOD performs. Jesus is our High Priest standing in the Presence of GOD making intercession for the Church; adding His perfection fragrance and excellence to our prayers **[Hebrew 7:25]. Yeshua tells us in [Matthew 26:28] This is my blood of covenant which is poured out for the many for the forgiveness of sins.** The Blood Covenant: for our guilt and poverty He gave us His innocence and riches… for our judgment He gave us His mercy… He reverse the curse and He blesses. The Blood of JESUS gives the believing soul eternal virtue in a hostile world. Our High Priest entered not into the Holy Place made by man hands, which was a copy of the true tabernacle, HEAVEN, but into the Presence of the Father for us with His untainted, holy, unblemished, perfect blood and eternal life once and for all times **[Hebrew 5:9-10; 9:11, 21-24]**. Just as the high priest in **Leviticus 16** sacrificed unblemished animals, a foreshadow, JESUS is the unblemished Lamb of GOD slaughtered for us, the Lamb that not only protects His own through His blood, but He is the Azazel (scapegoat) that takes away the sins, as far as the east is from the west, of those who will partake of the grace by drawing near to GOD.

JESUS is the truth, the life and the way (the Gate) of the tabernacle **[John 14:6]**. He is the only access to the heavenly Father and the entrance authorized by faith which is demonstrated in obedience grounded in love. It's the divine nature of the blood that carries this new life thought (DNA) and makes the supernatural actuality a reality in chronos; earthly time zones. The Blood of JESUS puts to death the works of carnality and its appetite… the old man. The Blood of Jesus stimulates the supernatural sphere of GOD. The Blood of Jesus gives access and power. The Blood of Jesus can reach… name it… it reaches that too. The Blood of Jesus is the healer of heart sickness, the body and mind disease. The Blood of Jesus is healing for every ailment that appears. What appears on the surface is a result of what's in the heart of man. The blood's power, the blood's authority goes beneath the surface to the conscience and soul to bring about supernatural revival. The blood reaches the innermost parts of our being; the soul, heart, thoughts, feelings and the mind. The Blood of JESUS leaves nothing unclean or unprofitable. JESUS blood makes the spots, the blemishes, the strongholds, the temptation and the sins vanish from the heart with no appetite or residue for regrowth. The Blood of Jesus! JESUS blood keeps us saved and sanctified and healed and restored in the mind, spirit and body. He makes you whole. The Blood of JESUS positions the believer in a priestly royal estate **[1 Peter 2:9]**. We are given access to boldly approach the throne of grace confidently in time of need **[Hebrew 4:16]**. As a priest you are ordained of GOD through the Spirit to be a living sacrifice, pure and holy. As a priest you are commissioned to seek GOD in prayer. It's through the Spirit of Christ that our minds are renewed with eternal things for manifestation. As priest our spiritual garment is to be undefiled. The Blood of Christ gives us virtuous garments and consumes the unrighteous, stained garment. As a priest our sacrifice to the LORD as a sweet smelling aroma includes our lifestyle, our speech, our worship, our motives, how we serve, treat others and family or the stranger.

Now that we have a clearer understanding of the holiness of the blood sacrifice in the next few paragraphs we're going to look further into forgiven grace state of mind. Forgiven grace changes our spiritual condition; the atmosphere of the soul and provides us with more than what we deserve. Forgiven grace renews a right spirit and a clean heart within the repentant **[Psalm 51:10]**. The state of forgiven isn't applied for the sake of the CROSS, but for the sake of removing the partition that separates man from GOD; to restore covenant union **[Luke 1:77]** and to destroy all that plagues… that locks up the soul. The divine spiritual bill of right "Forgiven" is unconditional love exposed in favor and mercy. Because this principle is already done, set in motion, irreversible this same principle meets a soul at anytime in any place in life to deposit its liberation renewal, authority and peace. Although forgiven is filled with grace, favor, love and the mercies of Almighty GOD already completed at the CROSS, it doesn't tolerate or legalized acts of treason, but this divine principle empowers believers to triumph over disloyalty with acts of purity. We must comprehend this spiritual truth. Visualize your flesh being nailed on the cross instead of the one who traded places because of our unworthiness and shortage. There had to be a CROSS to bear the crime of iniquity and transgression that was more than able to meet all righteous and holy decrees and return to Glory with keys signifying all authority, only access and power for a believer not only to possess, but demonstrate the life of royalty and dominion. That dominion is authorized to close doors that can present themselves in the believer's new life in the future. The Fire of the LORD which authorizes dominion destroys generational patterns and assaults sent against your posterity, liberty, mind and emotions. This activation is spiritual first then natural.

GOD is gracious, affectionate and full of unfailing unconditional love. It is His nature to love like this. It's all for His sake and from His court of justice. We are powerless to do anything to provoke this type of love. **The Bible tells us in [Isaiah 43:25] I, even, I am he who blots out your transgressions, for my own sake and remembers your sins no more.** How great is our GOD, who is able to give new life and preserve the body and the soul from eternal hell fire. Forgiven grace breaks the chain completely. GOD condemned what condemned you eternally by His promise to blot out every sin under the sun that one can ever do or have done. GOD, who is holy takes honor and pleasure to pardon, release and grant anyone that is captive to be "set free". Yahweh promised after blotting the sins out for His righteous sake that He will not remember them no more... He forgets our mess... our corruption. Father GOD does not bring up our past sins to us, so why return or resume to a life that once was in bondage to repeat its death cycle. He does not remember them. Yet, that doesn't give us an excuse to practice or dabble in sin or play with temptation. If you bring it up or return back to the filth the stench reaches His nostrils for judgment. We are either hot or cold, in or out of His will; receive GOD or reject GOD. There is no middle ground. GOD knows the intent of the heart. The heart and mouth must speak the same language the language of heaven. Yahweh unmerited favor is not cheap nor does it gives one the permission or assumption that it's okay to do as you please without ramification. Any bait the tempter uses has a hidden intention to catch its prey with hooks attached. **The Bible tells us in [Hebrew 8:12] it is confirmed what God spoke to the prophet Isaiah: For I will forgive their wickedness and will remember their sins no more. Another translation says I will not hold their sins against them.** GOD does not hold our past against us, but satan holds it and will keep your past in your mind. He will always bring up your past for entrapment; it's his nature. The past is just what it means, that which you are done with, have repented of, have turned your back to and have reconciled your differences in order to set your slate clean with GOD and others according to His plumb line.

GOD confirms again to us in the verse above that which He had already spoken to the prophet in the Old Testament is relevant today through the Blood of Jesus. This is an expression of an everlasting love for those belonging to Him through covenant, the blood of Christ relation. Therefore, Yeshua fills a believer's soul with His Holy Spirit. The curse that was holding one in guilt and shame is broken through his unfailing love shown through his bloody bruised body hanging from that bloody cross. It takes the working of the Word of GOD to awaken us spiritually in order to see with spiritual soberness when one may be in a state of captivity. It's a good thing to see reality than to live life in a lie. Seeing and judging matters at heart righteously are the first steps in the direction of freedom in that area(s). If one falls into temptation from the frailty of the flesh, **the Bible tells us in [1 John 1:9] If we confess our sins he is faithful and just to forgive us of our sins and cleanse us from all unrighteousness.** The Blood gives a new heart transfusion; the heart of the Father and the heart of sonship. The blood makes this transaction available and fruitful. Fruitfulness that is evidence of the work that Holy Spirit has began within. He will complete it the same way He started it which is by His Holy Spirit. Salvation is the work of the Spirit by faith. Sanctification is by the work of the same Spirit in the new life and eternal redemption is by work of the Spirit of Christ. Spiritual fullness in Christ declares a soul redeemed and free to experience righteousness, peace with GOD, birthright blessings and the inner capability to live by the grace virtues and experience the Glory of GOD. Remember, the measure of fullness of life comes from GOD and is Christ life in you. The CROSS Act of Mercy and Grace is never to be taken lightly, but understood as divine blessings for whosoever will come and remain… understood as the only way for spiritual rebirth, understood as the power to sonship, understood as an altar experience for carnality to be put to death, understood as victory over defeat, understood as vengeance on all unrighteousness, understood as vengeance on the Kingdom of darkness, understood as the believer victory and understood as receiving the King's inheritance.

The Law of Christ buys back souls, gives the soul a clean slate from the past life once lived along with favor and imparts the Kingdom of GOD into the believing soul… ruling power of the Holy Spirit. It is the only supernatural bill of right that can delete every charge and accusation made against us through the Law of the Spirit-Christ and set you free from the ordinances that stand against you; the law of sin and death **[Romans 8:2]**. The phrase the law of sin and death means 1) separation from God 2) spiritual death 3) then physical death. Physical death doesn't always come immediately. The law cannot guarantee freedom's worth to anyone who say they partake of its constitution, but remains or routinely deny the criterion (condition) of the Law of Christ or continue to live in sin after receiving and understanding the knowledge of Truth. This is trampling in the Blood of Christ (trample the Son of GOD underfoot, insulting the grace of glory) rendering it non effective to meet the soul spiritual need for redemption, cleansing and sanctification. **The Bible tells us in [Hebrew 10:27, 29-31] But only a fearful expectation of judgment and a raging fire that will consume the enemies of God. How much more severely do you think someone deserves to be punished who has trampled the Son of God underfoot, who has treated as an unholy thing the blood of the covenant that sanctified them and who has insulted the Spirit of grace. God said, it is my to avenge; I will repay, the Lord will judge his people. It is a dreadful thing to fall into the hands of the living God.** God is not mocked nor can He be deceived or bewitched. He is not bipolar, absent minded or influenced from anything outside of Himself; we reap what we sow. Anything that forces itself against our birthright in Christ is to be overthrown by the authority of the Word of GOD through obedience just as Christ overturned the tables in the synagogue **[Matthew 21:13]** for unrighteous acts-treason-rebellion… grace demoters. This is serious soul searching business and includes attacks on the mind.

The Spirit of Christ gives life, promotes life, sustains life and authorizes its wellbeing and citizenship; this is the revelation of no more shackles and no more chains. Forgiven grace doesn't put force or pressure upon no one, but it is a privileged sacrifice for any soul to partake of the course of its divine nature... Christ nature. Divine favor "Grace" is never to be thought of as a one time only experience. Unmerited favor never stops producing in the life of the faithful believing believer. The believer's development, maturity... perfection is a continuous practice because favor is continuous... grace is continuous; and the Church must long for a continuous outpour of the Holy Spirit... wholeness. Remember, divine favor is promotional in the Kingdom of GOD; it causes increase in more ways than one. Grace calls and positions us in the new spiritual state and grace manifests the new state through the working of Holy Spirit. Grace nature next ingredients causes' soul elevation in Christ. Because forgiven grace positions the soul in the godly position of holiness and righteousness, grace nature teaches you how to battle according to the Spirit to conquer, discern and master sin's seduction; meaning we fight a difference fight in a different sphere with grace strength and favor to triumph in this physical realm over what has already been conquered through the Blood of Yeshua. The fight believers fight charges the atmosphere to loose what is yours and to bind what is unlawful. One way of fighting is by asking Holy Spirit to grace you in this matter... whatever your matter maybe... you're asking for supernatural acceleration and reinforcement to live on. We must study, mediate, activate and practice the Word of GOD in faith to conquer by faith. Divine favor causes the spiritual blessings of GOD to swell or overtake the faithful and obedient. Grace and favor seeks no permission from mankind to perform; these twins express the will of the Father to His faithful ones. Receive the knowledge of Holy Spirit.

As the Word of GOD swells in our soul like a woman with child, the Holy Spirit enthrones from within, we're increasing for kingdom manifestation. Let the swelling of the understanding of the Word of GOD -His Mind- be the plan and strategy for overcoming all that seek to oppress your mind, steal your focus, peace, all that rises to take you out of character or sonship. This can happen through desensitization... bits and bits and pieces and bits... making the soul less sensitive or doubtful toward God's Word, Presence and Spirit. ABBA promotes through His righteousness and He sees believers clothed in the rank of sonship through His only begotten Son... JESUS the CHRIST. Sonship of the body of Christ speaks of Christ likeness, discipline, character, relation, wisdom, position, experiential truth, spiritual maturity and adoption through the blood participating in the inheritance benefits as sons (no gender) in the family of GOD; children of the Promise. The spiritual sons (positional) have legal right to all the Father has for us until the fullness of our sonship reward at the second coming of Christ. These are those who are filled with the Spirit [**Acts 13:52**]. These are those who can identify and refuse to bow to the works of deception and darkness [**James 4:7**]. The sons are they who walk in the Spirit, see darkness, see deception, experience pain and suffering, experience frustration and worry; yet, because of the revelation of the power of the Holy Spirit they chose to remain in covenant agreement through obedience [**Psalm 119:105**]. These are those who repent of their wrongdoing, learn from it and walk in the light [**Psalm 56:13**]. These are they who are taught by the Holy Spirit to run into ABBA's presence and to remain faithful in loyalty in spite of what approaches the feelings. These are they who are not only hearers, but doers of the Word of GOD. The sons of GOD are they who are led by the Spirit of GOD [**Romans 8:14**]. The sons of GOD are they who make it a lifestyle to hearken to the Will of GOD. These are they that don't shrink back, but arm themselves in the spirit daily by putting on the whole armor of GOD. These are they that meditate on the Word and seek the Lord [**Psalm 1:1-3**]. These are they who practice continuously to surrender their will in obedience to Christ. These are they who surrender to Him as their personal Master. These are they who are Holy Ghost trained to suffer for the sake of suffering with Christ [**2 Timothy 2:12**]. These are they who are being stripped of self for (Jesus) righteousness sake. These are they who have been buried with Jesus in baptism and raised with Him from the dead by faith in Messiah [**Colossians 2:12**]. The sons of GOD are they who are in love with Messiah JESUS. The sons (no gender) are those who live in the revelation that I am nothing without Him and with Him I can do all things [**John 15:5**]. The sons of GOD are they who stay connected to and remain in the True Vine.

Romans 8:13-15

Therefore, brethren, we are debtors not to the flesh, to live after the flesh. For if ye live after the flesh, ye shall die: but if ye live through the Spirit do mortify the deeds of the body, ye shall live. For as many as are led by the Spirit of God, they are the sons of God. For ye have not receive the spirit of bondage again to fear; but ye have received the Spirit of adoption, whereby we cry, Abba, Father.

Galatians 4:6-7

And because ye are sons, God hath sent forth the Spirit of his Son into your hearts, crying Abba, Father. Therefore thou art no longer a slave, but a son, and if a son then and heir through Christ.

Therefore, believers in Christ must consider through "Forgiven Grace" conquering the "I" syndrome that will demand its place on the throne of our hearts after we have received Christ as Lord and Savior. Knowing the Law of Christ and applying the Law of Christ are two different tasks and both can be challenging. The body of Christ has been endowed with Holy Ghost power to push. The eternal power *kratos* gives authorized power *dunamis* to the Spirit-filled believer to push which produces a spiritual conception, pleasure and freedom. This directive is carried out through understanding sonship (positional) reality... sons like Father GOD' *(the Law of the Spirit is another title expression for the Law of Christ and Spirit of Christ)*. First you must agree that "I" have to be dethroned off of the heart and bow to Christ wholeheartedly. This is part of growing spiritually mature in the LORD through the perfecting work of the Spirit of Christ. Remember, the body of Christ never stops expanding in Christ in this life time; in the flesh yes, but in the Spirit of Christ no and in sonship no. The Church never arrives fully on this side, but we flourish in and by Him. The Spirit of GOD has so much to reveal, teach and demonstrate to us and through us in our new life on earth. As "I" humble itself then, the stature of sonship moves forward to connect with Father and Holy Spirit. Although the concept is spiritual, that which is spiritual will be clothe and manifest through our members: body, tongue, hands, feet, mouth, eyes, ears and/ or our presence which means the more "I" surrender to the LORD, the Spirit of Christ will cause the Christ in me to bring my flesh into subjection to the Spirit of Christ who conquers. As "I" yield the more Christ in me (you) rules. The more "I" keep my mind stayed on GOD by submitting the Christ in me will purge my thoughts; strengthen His wisdom in my inner-man so that I in Christ will have a revelation of His peace. The more "I" set my affections on things above the less worldliness I will desire and the Christ in me will satisfy my taste with the kingdom appetite. The more "I" feed my inner-man the Word of GOD the more supernatural substance of the Spirit will the Christ in me enlarge in my inner-man to live and do the will of the Father. The more "I" feed my inner-man the Word of GOD the new man begotten of Christ is sharpened by the Holy Spirit to be keen in the realm of the spirit for Kingdom purposes. The more "I" draw close to the LORD the Christ in me bond is made stronger and the "I" in Christ become unified with the Spirit in heart, word and deed. The more "I" feed my inner-man the Word of GOD the more sensitive I will become to kingdom blessings. The more "I" grow close to the LORD the new man in Christ learns to walk in the fear of the LORD, recognize, hear and heed the voice of the LORD, learn quickly to repent, forgive, practice patience and seek GOD. The more "I" draw close to the LORD the new man in Christ learns to humble self and not be anxious for things. Lastly, the more "I" surrender... move out of the way, the Light of Christ shines forth. As believers yield to Jesus the power of Holy Spirit develops and increases in the believer in the stature of sonship in six stages: 1) acceptance 2) learning 3) understanding 4) knowledge 5) practice and 6) discipline.

One of the tricks of the devil is to present lies that will build up fear within the soul in order to move you from the place of dominion, place of obedience or place of sonship; causing lack, feebleness in strength and to aim at your faith which produces trust in GOD. The spirit of fear will arrest a soul from making progress, causes one to respond by not responding in faith and paralysis one from moving forward in the promises of God such as achievements. Let's understand that closure to any problem is a step in the right direction, but will require healing sometimes in multiple areas that appeared through a single decision. The devil only steals through ignorance, the comfort zone, pride and association to the past. Ignorance is a choice with results; meaning one can choose not to submit, not to study the Word of God, not to pray or obey GOD, resist the adversary, love your neighbor as yourself, not to work or choose not to improve self. Yes, it is a choice. Our decisions determine our outcome. And what makes it a choice is the "response" we take toward any past or current issue relating to something in the past or present. For example: if we do something or nothing, grumble, disagree with the boss or spouse that's a reaction from the choice that was made. Ignorance is the lack of understanding information or knowledge about something; unaware of the whole truth. Incomplete or inaccurate information sown can reap a wrong decision followed by behavior; vice versa, accurate knowledge sown reaps a wholesome decision and behavior. The blessing is accurate knowledge that is active cancels out the lack of understanding. Where the lack of is corrected the people of GOD create, rise, do exploits and are revived in spirit by Truth. **The Bible tells us in [Daniel 11:32]... but the people that know their God shall stand (be strong) and take action (resist-prevail).** *The Hebrew word for know means to act justly by way of divine knowledge and understanding instructed by wisdom.* The name of the LORD alone bears greatness; the weight of His Glory and Fire. The name of the LORD is the name believers in Christ bear in righteousness and freedom. God's name manifests His character and nature in the spiritual and physical realm. God's name is a banner over the believer in Christ. Wherever the believer goes He is already there. God's name signifies His Presence, Holiness, Sovereignty, Reverence, Glory, Law, Agape, Revelation, Knowledge, Counsel, Faithfulness, Salvation, Abundance, Sanctification, Prosperity, Protection, Ownership, Covenant Provision, Guide, Salvation and Eternal Victory. We put our trust and hope in His name because He is our Covenant GOD and there is no failure or defeat or slumber in Him. Yeshua is the same yesterday, today and forever more **[Hebrew 13:8]**. He changes not. Yeshua is the First and the Last and the Creator of all. He is the Resurrection and the Bread of Life. GOD always rises to the occasion of defending His faithful and obedient; those that recognize, heed, return, trust and obey Him. This doesn't mean we are without mistakes, but it means your heart is in sink with the work of the Spirit within your soul and your willingness to submit and not walk in intentional sin. This results in taking responsibility for our actions at all times, practicing accountability, dedication, total alliance to the LORD, apt to serve, loving the unlovable, staying focus and praying. Actions are expressions of your decisions (choices) and are evidence of what is in the heart. Bearing the name of the LORD is honorable and rewarding for the souls that know their GOD. Having divine revelation and knowledge of who GOD is will paralyze the spirit of fear and cancel out lack. The works of the flesh are put to death; cancel the old contract of all that pertains to the old and darkness.

You are new and alive in Christ **[Romans 8:13-15; Colossians 3:5-9]**. There is a supernatural sphere authorized by Holy Spirit calling you to position yourself according to the grace that called, sanctioned and made all things new concerning you.

2 Corinthians 5:17
If any be in Christ the old has passed away
and behold, the new has come.

Revelation 3:11
Behold, I come quickly holdfast that which
thou hast that no man take your crown.

Ephesians 2:6
And God raised us up with Christ and seated us with him
in the heavenly realms in Christ Jesus in order that in the
coming ages he might show the incomparable riches of his
grace expressed in his kindness to us in Christ Jesus.

Although we are human (earthly, weak) the believer (spiritual) must see the revelation and vision ABBA availed in creation and established by way of the CROSS. Elohim breath His Breathe His GLORY into dust and the Bible says that man became a living being... glory carriers... shakers in the earth... world chargers... grace promoters... phenomenal in Christ. There is more to us than the natural eye sees or the human mind can comprehend. That which is spiritual is maintained by the Spirit of GOD. It takes the Word of GOD, the Power and the Fire of GOD to maintain this new life in Christ with the old life of "I" syndrome lying prostate before the LORD. The Spirit of GOD is life giving, life imparting and life establishing. Commit your will... your will unto the LORD daily (dethrones "I") through submission and trust. Without Christ we are incomplete, without Truth, without instruction, without covering and without divine identity which equates to chaos… corruption. When ones eyes, which represent vision, are taken off focus or out of love for GOD, the mind of the flesh (I-ego) will seek to rise, speak and dictate its desires to the body. The snare doesn't always appear to look bad, but wears a clever flattery disguise that can persuade the soulish sphere *(Psuche Greek word for soul: the will, intellect and emotions)* or to draw one's interest. This is the doorway that wrong persuasion or demonic influence can enter depositing its perceptions that will lead one astray; away from the CROSS into apostasy **[Genesis 3:4]**. Wrong persuasion can cause a soul to second guess GOD with what "sounds" right or what make sense to the five senses without questioning it.

The Bible refers to flesh as carnality or the carnal mind [the five senses which are connected to this physical realm]. Other names that refer to the flesh are the old man, sinful nature, old nature, earthly mind or worldly mind and unspiritual. The flesh can overrule the Spirit by feeding its earthly appetite through influence of foolishness, entertaining carnal notions (worldly wisdom), stubbornness, not knowing the Word of GOD, not being filled with the Holy Spirit and by rejecting God's holy Word. All that's within the carnal mind that compels a soul to live or indirectly agree with temptation, compromise and avoid God's wisdom are manifestations evolved from the heart's stubbornness and blindness to sin; thinking that conceives to exalt itself above or against the knowledge of God's Truth. Such doors will lead to the sin of omission, bondage and perversion. It is the working of the mind of the Spirit of Christ plus submission within the soul that overrules carnality, the worldly mind or unspiritual mind. The carnal mind can be a breathing ground, an open door, for spiritual enslavement to sin and temptation. **The Bible tells us in [Proverbs 16:6] By mercy and truth iniquity is purged and by the fear of the LORD men depart from evil.** Listed are eight major strategies how bondage and temptation can be overruled in a believer's soul and trampled under foot: 1) hearing the voice of GOD 2) recognizing the voice of GOD 3) obeying the voice of GOD 4) believing GOD will still speak to you 5) desiring that GOD speak to you continually 6) open communion with GOD that stirs up and strengthens an ongoing personal fellowship 7) fellowship that causes a deep reverence and fear of the LORD 8) a heart that will not compromise this luxury and crown. Hearing and recognizing the voice of GOD will establish a sobering bond. Whenever the Spirit of GOD speaks that within itself will arrest and interrupt your skills, language, plans, intellect and comprehension. It brings your will and understanding to zilch. Desire and ask GOD to speak to you. He is waiting for your hunger to spiritually hear what He has been saying all along. Keep a journal close by. He speaks in a variety of ways.

You will have no words to explain or describe the encounters that He wants to become a norm for the body of Christ. You must seek and safeguard this kingdom increase which comes through denying yourself and taking up your cross to follow Christ.

Even though there is a continual conflict between the regenerated nature (Law of the Spirit) and the degenerated nature (law of the flesh-soul) the believer is to recognize it, judge it and prevail over it. **The Bible tells us in [Romans 7:18] For I know that in me (that is in my flesh) dwells no good thing: for to will is present with me: but how to perform that which is good I find not. V23 But I see another law in my members, warring against the law of my mind and bringing me into captivity to the law of sin which is in my members.** Remember, the freedom believers obtain in Christ is manufactured by the Holy Spirit. Holy Spirit and the Word of GOD is the how to, to perform what the law of the old man cannot. No one can walk this walk without the sufficiency of His grace. God's grace sufficiency is that it extends beyond any boundary... it extends and extends and extends. And His grace is not only spiritual, but naturally performs itself by resting upon hearts to perform that which is good and perfect in the sight of GOD in our lives. God's divine grace is indescribable and beyond details; it's a soul encounter experience. The Law of the Spirit of Christ who gives this new life cares and creates what is of Him within our spirit. The Law of the Spirit gives us a new heart with new desires with new persuasions for possessing more of Him. A few spiritual blessings of desiring to obtain more of Him are ears to hear, eyes to see and a conscious mind to live Christ... pursuing the knowledge and wisdom of Christ **[Philippians 1:21]**. This freedom rouses active faith persuasion in your life that unction's determination to conquer bondage that we might overcome the lust of the eyes, lust of the flesh and the pride of life... overcome weaknesses. The LORD gives us a new will, new assignments, new position, new territories, new directions, new beginnings, new ideas and deletes desires that do not belong to the new creature in Christ; and deletes persuasion that's not in His will for you... remember submission is a key factor. Neither the old nor the past has know place in the new. Neither the old nor the past can gravitate to the divine intelligences of the new. As Apostle Paul stated, I see another law in my members... the war in the law of my mind that works bondage [**Romans 7:23**]. The old nature's mind is connected to unrestrained lusts and the new nature's mind is connected to dominion intelligences through the will of the Father in Christ; in the mind of the Spirit dwells every good thing.

Bear in mind, its Christ nature now that lives within you as a believer. We house His Spirit and His Spirit's nature can give us the world (harmony, wholesomeness) as we seek His Kingdom first. Life in Christ is more than being blessed with material or earthly possessions. The Kingdom of GOD teaches the royal priesthood how to walk-live in this land, conduct business, resolve issues, how to live victorious, how to demonstrate His love grace toward others, how to live wisely, as well as holy, how to persevere in faith, contend for the faith, how to be content, manage, stewardship and more. We carry the greater substance within us to help others and to perform at a higher standard from a higher dimension with a new tongue (Kingdom) in the workplace, with family, outsiders and in our personal lives. Grace dimension instructs the Church to operate from its standard which is of another dimension; unlike the world. The devil will use anything and anybody to sabotage this measure of freedom grace. Remember, the mind of the flesh and the mind of the Spirit of Christ both use the body as its function, but different spheres of the supernatural. The Holy Spirit (supernatural) is available only by GOD and His Truth and is the attraction to the Seed of Christ which lives within each believing believer. The mind of the flesh opened to the earthly notions can be like a magnet in the realm of the spirit. Remember, the mind has the involuntary capability to connect in the spirit realm.

Ekklesia (Called out of darkness, light ones, body of Christ) rise up and take your proper place as authorized citizens of the Kingdom of GOD. It's Time to Wake Up body of Christ! We are saved and baptized with fire with a divine function and a divine position. We are restored, marked in Christ with the seal of the promised Holy Spirit until the day of redemption **[Ephesians 1:14]. The Bible tells us in [Romans 8:1-4] There is now no condemnation for those who are in Christ Jesus, who walk <u>not</u> after the flesh, but after the Spirit. For what the law was powerless to do because it was weakened by the flesh, GOD did by sending his own Son in the likeness of sinful flesh to be a sin offering in the flesh. That the righteousness of the law might be fulfilled in us, who walk <u>not</u> after the flesh, but after the Spirit.** The flesh has a mind and the Spirit has a mind. We must take into account that when one falls short to take ownership of our actions, acknowledge the errant way and REPENT; only then, does this promise offers an open door for manifesting forgiven benefits without being judge or condemned by Yeshua (Jesus), as the Ruach Hakodesh (Holy Spirit) performs His work inwardly.

Yahweh cleanses and restores the soul because of His constitution of love. The sin-carnal nature will be with us until death, but the Church, which is born of the Spirit of Christ, is given ordained authority over the law of the mind of the flesh. Condemnation is the opposite of Grace. Condemnation is rooted in the spirit of fear and guilt and shame; which is attached to the past. The spirit of condemnation seeks to keep you connected to your past, bring up your past and makes one rethink to return to their past. Condemnation screams shame and guilt screams dishonor and disgrace... but grace arrests the scream of guilt and shame and all of its dark shadows. Grace screams worthiness and clothes us with worthiness in the blood of Yeshua. Grace gives believers supernatural spiritual vitality to look up, look forward and move in the predestined plan of GOD. It is the power awareness of "I CAN IN CHRIST" "I AM IN CHRIST" And "I WILL IN CHRIST." That's walking in the Spirit. Walking in the Spirit is a spiritual awakening of the soul out of its sleep to grace consciousness, grace effectiveness, grace awareness and grace open-mindedness. The very act of forgiven grace is also the very effective power of the arm of the LORD. Grace judgment speaks the Father's mind through Christ. Grace immerses the believer into the sphere of favor, beauty, acts of kindness, forgiveness and a good return. This supernatural strength of character and favor of the LORD empowers the believing soul to walk close to the Lord in the conscience of spirit and soul. Holy Spirit teaches us how to be GRACE conscious as we keep our hearts focused on the finished works JESUS have prepared for the believer through His blood and His righteousness.

There is a change and a supernatural holy charge in the soul of a person when the soul shifts to bow down and the conscience is awakened by the Holy Spirit. GOD forgiven (freedom) grace covers every aspect of our life and works to perfect all that concerns you from personal needs, spousal indifferences, divorce, remarriage, the single life, godly dating, prayer, relationships, college, grand-children, retirement, health, finances, restraints, where to locate or move, where to work, troubles, discussions, plans, dreams, adventures, future, desires, goals and etc **[Psalm 138:8]**. Heavenly Father is concerned about all that concerns you. In all that we encounter the soul is only made whole in the LORD. **The Bible tells us in [John 6:63] It is the Spirit that gives life; the flesh profits nothing; the words that I have spoken to you are spirit and life.** Only because of Jesus Christ the soul has life filled with hope and fruitfulness. **The Bible tells us in [Proverbs 24:16a] a just (upright in the LORD) man (a soul) falls seven times and rises up again...** the focus here is not on the number of times, but on the active power of grace that is sufficient in that dark place that draws one to turn back to GOD;

that we rise up out of the pit of darkness by the power of the CROSS. Grace is there to rescue the returning heart. However, on the other hand we should not be repeating the same struggles over and over; Christ reveals the mystery to His body (the Church) through the power of accountability and the power of elevation (Cross). The Church focus is up… victory bound in Christ; persevere for victory manifestation.

Commit this to heart: a believer in Christ, choices and decisions are established in Christ through the finished work of the CROSS. Think about it! The new man in Christ governs and creates by the new mind and the new appetite… Christ life. The Holy Spirit teaches us to choose the will of the Yahweh. This manifests as earthly minds are renewed in Christ. Apostle Paul directs the Church, believers in Christ, to let the mind of Christ be in you and be not conformed to this world, but be "transformed" by the "renewing" of your mind. **The Bible tells us in [Romans 12:2 NIV] And be not conformed to this world; but be ye transformed by the renewing of your mind**. Conforming to the world is dangerous. This is extremely powerful because the mind and the heart share relation. They function spiritually dependent on each other. We think the way we think due to what is in the heart. We act the way we act because of what is in the heart and mind. The mind and the heart change when they are transformed and conform by the Power of the Word through the renewing process. When the mind is renewed the heart changes. When the heart is responsive to the renewing it conforms to the change. Renewing (law of attraction) is a powerful tool for guarding the heart. Renewing the mind is like getting rid of all old furniture including wall pictures, fixtures, wallpaper or paint and such like. Then, filling the room with new and vibrant furniture; the room is now fully renovated (made alive) with new ideas. The renewing of the mind with Christ thoughts deletes the earthly concepts that aren't beneficial to the new creature and bring in His kingdom concepts. You are a king and a priest of GOD (spiritual, no gender) [**Revelation 1:6; 5:10**]. And the mind of a king and a priest is fixed in godliness in its decisions. *Transformed comes from two words Metaschematizo (change and appearance) and Metamorphoo (change, appearance and characteristics) which mean a total change, an unceasing and progressive spiritual change in the image of GOD by the power of the Holy Spirit; a change from within through a supernatural reality. Meta means change… trans means across over and form means from.* We cannot bring about a change without Holy Spirit interference. Change comes from remaining connected to the power source through the blood of Jesus. When a Christian's mind is being made new it is through the indulging and entrance of God's Word, prayer, loyalty, commitment and fellowship which all work together to continually transform our lives. *Conformed comes from the Greek word Suschematizo which means to outward model what is seen, fashion and shape one's self according to another's pattern. Schema means* everything within a person which strikes the carnal senses. The Church is to take the form (mind and character) of GOD as sons *(summorphizo: growing into conformity, death in Christ, death to the carnal self)* and not conform to the pattern of this world *(suschematizo: changeable, unstable)* concepts, lifestyles, darkness and ungodly laws. We have to surrender and allow ourselves to be changed; changed in substance and form; the mind. Just as the caterpillar undergoes change to become that beautiful, unique butterfly in the same way Christ works in us. When He is allowed by the soul to bring change, transformation by His Fire, you will not desire to return back to your former lifestyle. Just as the butterfly no longer returns to the caterpillar state or have a desire too. This is manifested from experiencing an encounter with Christ that makes this a reality. The Fire of GOD burns out the old appetite and births the new appetite.

If a believer follows after the spirit of the world which we were set apart, it opens the door to lukewarm behavior; a life apart from GOD [**Galatians 5:19-21**]. It takes the Holy Spirit and the Fire of the Spirit to rid the soul of practices and residues that defiles the temple. For example: smokes and liquor defiles the temple (you), as well as, stealing, sex before marriage, bad tempter, misery or discord... lukewarm spirit. In the world believers in Christ are aliens, strangers and an enemy to it. JESUS was the example of a nonconformist... our example. **The Bible tells us in [1 John 2:15-16] Do not love the world or anything in the world. If anyone loves the world the love of the Father is not in him. For everything in the world the craving of sinful man, the lust of his eyes and the boasting of what he has and does comes not from the father but from the world.** This is blunt, straight forward love from the Father. It is impossible to love the world and GOD at the same time... impossible. This is what the scripture verse refers to in **2 Corinthians 4:4** satan is the prince of the air; another translation god of this world... meaning the system in operation and ungodly practices. To love the world means to be in intimate fellowship and agreement with it, devoted to it values, ways and taking pleasure in what is offensive to GOD or opposes Him. Loving the world will pollute your companionship with GOD and will lead to spiritual destruction. *The Greek word for world is kosmos means the system of the world that satan promotes and the system that is independent of GOD combined with demonic and man's wisdom.* This system also includes secret organizations, man-made rights, laws and man-made unbiblical-godless religion systems. The world system, to name a few, that satan uses: government, music, education, entertainment, technology, mass media, religion, sports, philosophies, psychology, science, farming (legalizing mind-life destroying drugs) and medical (killing unborn babies), etc, whether at a lesser or greater degree. BREAK The CHAIN!

The Church, as the temple of GOD [**1 Corinthians 3:16-17**], is to be aware and not indulge or get caught up in the hype of things. Since there is an unseen realm, we must be aware that behind all human endeavors there is an existing unseen power that opposes GOD. And since it opposes GOD, it also opposes that which GOD created in His image for His will, pleasure and purpose, but that power does not exist under Christ Lordship. The believer in Christ is not to fear; although we see this power in operation today. The agenda of the world system will oppose GOD and remove Him from the seen completely. This will come, but not in good taste or peace… called the Great Tribulation. We are not to allow the ideas and influences of today change us and this is accomplished by remaining connected in loyalty and fellowship. The opposite is separation which results in loss of fellowship with GOD [**2 Corinthians 6:16**], loss of acceptance by the Father [**2 Corinthians 6:17**] and loss of birthright [**2 Corinthians 6:18; Romans 8:15-16**]. The world which is temporary will be destroyed by GOD [**2 Peter 3:10-12; Revelation 18:2**]. We must have an understanding, a revelation of who we are, whose we are and what our purpose is. As believers in Christ, we are called to be different by the one who is different and not to disguise our light to blend in with or adapt to darkness… this eventually terminates the light and salt. We are called by the Lord of Glory out of a dying world that's needs the Hope to be alive in it. And we have the Hope living within clay; the grace moral fiber that defines the believers in Christ as royal and peculiar. GOD called the Church to be set apart from the patterns of this world.

When all else fails or seem to go the wrong way because of the Hope and faith, we stand firm, let the Light shine from within and fight the good fight of faith… this why you're called by GOD as being peculiar and priestly. *Peculiar comes from the Greek word meaning a preserving.* **The Bible tells us in [Proverbs 3:26] For**

the LORD shall be thy confidence and shall keep thy foot from being taken. That which is being preserved is being kept in a supernatural, godly way that will maintain its renewed state, override toxic waste and won't become tainted over time by outside influence... preserving. **The Bible tells us in [Proverbs 2:10-12] When wisdom enter into the heart and knowledge is pleasant unto thy soul, discretion shall preserve thee, understanding shall keep thee. To deliver you from the way of the evil man, from the man that speaks forward (perverse) things.** Holy Spirit preserves His chosen, sets us apart to be holy by His blood and Spirit and keeps (preserves) believing believers from the deterioration that surrounds us. **The Bible tells us in [Psalm 121:8] The LORD will preserve thy going out and thy coming in from now unto eternity.** Because Holy Spirit sets us apart, we must agree to grow in the equity of holiness and discipline. It's a character trait in the royal blood of JESUS. Your faith will help your walk of holiness. This doesn't mean we get it right every single time, but it certainly means the believer's heart should be certain about the Hope that lives within the heart which is to be greater than the taste of the carnal nature that is to stay on the altar. **The Bible tells us in [Proverbs 4:23-24] Keep (guard) your heart with all diligence (vigilance) for out of it flow the issues of life. Put away from thee a forward mouth and perverse (deceitful) lips put far from thee.** The double heart (split soul - two faces) works hypocrisy... the soul that has heard Truth, experience Truth and know Truth; yet, lives both worlds. The singleness of heart is that soul that is continuously committing and submitting to GOD, fears GOD with a deep reverence, learning how to own up to personal mistakes, loving others in spite of and don't practice making excuses. The double heart same as a double mind is unstable in all its ways; therefore, in prison in the mind. Grace Breaks The CHAIN! The singleness of heart is a soul that is choosing to take the back seat, humbly surrender and giving the Holy Spirit the front seat to steer the soul.

The heart like the mind is the seat for self-consciou[s] directing, inner conviction and possession of thought tha[t] our reasoning, character and body and actions. **The Bi[ble tells] us in [Jeremiah 17:9] the heart is deceitful above all [things] and desperately wicked: who can know it?** GOD is th[e] one who can fix the heart, remove self deception and wicke[dness] that springs from a hard heart by the soul surrendering their [will]. Such hearts are blind to the truth by choice of stubbornness t[hat] can spawn from the spirit of rejection. This is what is revealed [by] being a blind choice (actions birth from thoughts, not words tha[t] speak what is or has been suppressed). The heart hides behind its foolishness and does not see itself or desires not to see itself. When the heart is blind it blinds the soul steps from being ordered by the LORD. However, each soul is a distinctive individuality; our creator, the Savior, Himself who knows our hearts can enter into our experiences to grace us. In such matters, the Church must intercede that the understanding of the heart be made to see and receive truth. **The Bible tells us in [Proverbs 25:4] Take out the dross from the silver and there shall come forth a vessel for the finer.** That power source is through the CROSS, the work of the Ruach (Spirit) of GOD and the Fire of Holy Spirit will make the vessel honorable, beautiful and fit for use by the Master. When one's way is ordered by God's way and not the other way around that's knowledge of understanding the wisdom of the LORD and acceptance of His instructions to lead.

STRATEGIES FOR
GUARDING YOUR HEART

...t of salvation

...our heart

...e of God rule in your heart

...sdom

...ous for nothing

...t, Don't hold grudges

...on the Mind of Christ

...ear fruit of forgiveness

Pray the Word of God

10. Seek to enter His Presence
11. Confess all hidden secrets of the heart to God
12. Seek God's approval not man
13. Guard your gates (body, ears, eyes, mouth, nose, hands, feet)
14. Govern your speech
15. Be watchful of the company you keep
16. Trust in the Lord with all your heart, mind and soul
17. Lean not to your own understanding
18. Acknowledge God in all that you do
19. In all that you do, do as a representative unto the Lord
20. Serve God faithfully
21. Shun evil communication and cast down evil imaginations
22. Resist compromise and temptations
23. Cast every concern upon the Lord
24. Meditate on the Word of God day and night
25. Persevere in faith

Nothing takes GOD by surprise. GOD knows all things and has taken all things into consideration through the Power of the CROSS, His Word and His Spirit; to bring the soul into alignment by His Spirit. No one will have an excuse in the court room before the judge. The condition of our heart-mind expresses to the desires of the flesh perception or the desires of the Spirit perception. Since Christ is the King that sits on the throne of a believer's heart our motives are placed in the examination room under a divine scope for spiritual surgery, qualification, approval and change by the Fire of Holy Spirit. We are to examine ourselves to rule out that which seeks to bring defilement from within. As we pass tests and overcome temptation we are growing and advancing as predestined in Christ; if we fail the test, a rebuke... correction... discipline is in order to bring God's divine order. Rebuke is good, as well as, correction and discipline. And when GOD speaks through His ordained messengers toward you; it's for disciplinary action and encouragement. Receive it and go in prayer to see what GOD is requiring of you. Stop getting offended when GOD, who is Spirit, corrects you through one of His sent vessels. Holy Spirit sees and Holy Spirit reveals ABBA wisdom to those He has entrusted with that measure of glory. Spirit of offense is demonic; it's not of GOD, but related to the sin of pride and witchcraft. The spirit of offense likened to the python spirit can slowly squeeze life out of soul, control one's emotions, desires, blur spiritual vision; cause lose of mental focus, panic attacks or compress one's breathing. GOD wills' the best for His children, just as parent desires the best for their child even when the child doesn't momentarily agree or understand completely. We still are responsible and held accountable by Holy Spirit to love hard by walking in the strength of GOD. ABBA loves hard (consequences for actions) bold, fearlessly, fiercely and with a holy jealousy (unlike carnal jealousy).

There are many in the Church building in bondage due to little understanding of the Fire of the Holy Spirit and their freedom right in salvation. Many have open unhealed wounds which have developed indirectly or directly; some by choices. Unhealed wounds can form unforgiveness, bitterness and form a camouflage… spirit of offense. Wounds, burdens weigh on the heart. We have a choice to let it go by faith and obedience "Release It" with the power of Holy Spirit or continue to carry the heavy load. We don't have to pick a fight in order to be involved, but if the heart co-signs with negative persuasion not only are you involved spiritually; you've secretly opened an unseen door in the spirit realm. If this isn't repented for and rebuked, that unseen door invites familiar spirits and over time they can manifest their assignment in that wounded soul. This mind has lent its mental power to the work of darkness without knowing or understanding what is really happening in the sphere of the emotions. That's a yoke. BREAK The CHAIN! Jehovah Rapha is our healer for all wounds and His anointing is like salve sealing the wound and what He heals, seals and anoints will supernaturally sprouts buds and blossoms… fruitfulness in your life. Holy Spirit is your comforter and teacher. He teaches us how to walk through the manifestation process of deliverance after receiving healing. (Purchase Bloodline Spiritual DNA, Identity).

Familiar spirits are spirits associated with one's bloodline (life line) in that family near or distance. In reality you are forgiven and Christ blood has already set the believer free even though the deliverance released from the heaven can be a process. All miracles don't occur over night. All deliverances don't take place at the same time. Some manifestations come quickly; while others do not, but GOD wants your whole heart forever through any duration of time. Time has nothing to do with faith. This is trust action in the finish work of the CROSS… activating the CROSS reality in your circumstances. Although, crisis or challenges will come up in your new life in Christ you have been given a measure of His Glory of victory for warfare by the Law of the Spirit. The devil schemes to pervert our thoughts during circumstances in order to target the believer to 1) lose strength and focus 2) lose vision and hope 3) to forfeit the birthright 4) to doubt the sacredness of being in Christ 5) to drown the truth of new life reality 6) to drown out the voice of GOD 7) to present the idea that the faith walk is too demanding and 8) the false idea that there's other paths to GOD. The liar and trickster, satan, instituted the same deception in the Garden of Eden with Mother Eve. Church, satan tactics haven't changed; his plans are defeated by the power of the CROSS and the Fire of the Spirit working in you and resting on those who obey and trust GOD. The Church must not sit idle, but recognize and discern satan's unrighteous tactics, persuasions and arrows sent to target the mind. The voice of GOD speaks greater in such times… the key is to practice being still to seek Him and listen.

We would think just because we're hidden then that's all to it, but in kingdom reality the believer in Christ must understand is the Kingdom concept for conception and application. Although Christ has hidden us we must recognize and agree with Truth in order to hide Truth in the inward parts of our soul for divine resistance, assistance and divine protection. Understanding the spiritual concept makes the heavenly reality a reality in time and space… a divine reality in time and in space. And when something is a reality we act with faith expectancy. GOD Said It! I Believe It! That's Final! It's shown through faith action. Divine assistance and divine resistance is not only the believer's power to resist the devil so that he will flee, but it is angelic reinforcement releasing the arrows of the LORD. It's Yeshua authority that gives believers the right to execute divine order far above all rule and authority, power and dominion and every name that is named not only in the present age, but also in the age to come **[Ephesians 1:18-23]. The Bible tells us in [Ephesians 2:6] And God raised us up with Jesus Christ and seated us in heavenly realms in Messiah.** Remember, as sons of GOD in Christ the life of the believer is Christ alive. Yes, we are human, but the Spirit of GOD we're infused with the supernatural power of the Holy Ghost. What is alive fills up space. Truth which is Spirit is hidden in the new mind can change the atmosphere, but a believer must be in agreement with the Kingdom of GOD divine perception pertaining to this life and godliness. Truth in the mind fills the space with GOD. GOD responds to His Word hidden in the heart not to the flesh or to the soul, but to His Word. Listen to the declaration of King David in **Psalm 119:11 Thy word have I hid in my heart that I might not sin against thee, LORD.** The Fire of the Holy Spirit brings the soul into submission and agreement. GOD can only respond to Himself hidden in our heart *(Hebrew word for heart: volition, mind, innerman)*. He breathes and grows Himself in the believer's heart by His Word, His Seed… Himself… which is the substance and mystery of Himself.

The heart is the picture of the human soul-spirit-mind; the soul we cannot physically see. It's joined to self, the seen and unseen and to loyalty. The conscience or the human spirit-soul (immaterial) is opened to the spirit world. Remember as stated before, the carnal mind feeds off of what is charged by the fives senses, the weakness of conscience or its deficiency reflects what the carnal mind perceives… when the soul is in charge; which can produce faulty understanding of scriptural truths and produce guilt and shame. **The Bible tells us in [Timothy 1:19] Cling to your faith and keep your conscience clear for some people have rejected or deliberately violated their conscience; as a result their faith is shipwrecked.** Thus far, we understand that the carnal -five senses- rely on what it physically can see, hear, touch, taste and smell. This is the reason our conscience (to know-moral judgment) must be renewed and transformed by the Word of GOD in order not to conform to worldliness or be weakened or defiled by wrong thoughts wrong persuasion… Christ in charge of the soul. When Christ is in charge of the soul, the Captain of the ship (will, emotions, thinking, actions), it is redirected for the greater good. Endurance and maturity in the faith strengthens the conscience (soul-heart). **The Bible tells us in [Hebrew 10:22] let us draw near with a sincere heart in full assurance of faith, having our hearts sprinkled clean from an evil conscience and our bodies washed with pure water.** As the heart and the Holy Spirit and the Word of GOD unite as one this creates a powerful union of command in the heavenly and the physical spheres. **The Bible tells us in [1 John 5:7-8] For there are three that testify on earth: the Spirit, the water and the blood; and these three are in agreement.** GOD has already given us Himself to duplicate His power in the earth realm. A powerful believer is one who knows without a doubt or second thought who they are in Christ and He is in them. This wisdom from GOD empowers the Ekklesia, the Church, to perform in ways that aren't common to man because the knowledge, understanding, endurance, training, equipping, skills, gifts, mantles, discernment, strength, determination and advancements come from the Spirit of the LORD and not man; divine holy alignment. Even though we become the target most importantly, understand all that targets royal, peculiar people of GOD is already defeated. We only receive revelation and strategy through understanding our destiny in the freedom that Christ has given at the cost of His life for ours. Yeshua (Jesus) takes those hidden in Him higher at the cost of dying to their life taking up their cross to follow Him no matter what the opposition is. GOD called the Church to a higher standard under the Blood Stain Banner of His everlasting love. The opposition which comes from beneath us has no power over us… the enemy is under your feet. Repeat that: THE OPPOSITION WHICH COMES FROM BENEATH US HAS NO POWER OVER US! Therefore; we must consistently and persistently walk close to GOD and abide in His present. Remember, He is the believer's High Tower. In Christ we inherited a promise in **Psalm 91:1** which is released through the Power of the finished work of the CROSS; the Blood of the Lamb of

GOD. The Blood of Yeshua carries the DNA -spiritual God-gene- of the body of Christ… spiritual identity for the holy nation in Christ.

Motives should be given to GOD who liberates and delete data that is not fit for the new creature restored state by the Law of the Spirit. The heart-mind can carry and hold motives developed from emotions. Emotions stirred up release motives (psychological state) that can influence the arousal of behavior or actions (physiological); good or bad. Our emotions release chemicals or energy that sends messages to our body… let that sink in… Emotions! Cells! Energy! Body! Reaction! Remember, our actions are a reflection of what is in our soul, thoughts or imagination. Doctor Jesus is the body of Christ Healer! Head! Breath and Thought! The mandate for the body of Christ is to trust GOD completely by casting every care upon Him; although challenging, allow these verses to breathe life to you. **The Bible tells us in [Hebrew 12:1-2 ISV] Therefore, since we are surrounded by such a great cloud of witnesses, let us throw off every thing that hinders and the sin that so easily entangles. And let us run with perseverance the race marked out for us, fixing our eyes on Jesus, the pioneer and perfecter of faith. For the joy that was set before him he endured the cross, scorning its shame and sat down at the right hand of the throne of God. The Bible tells us in [1 Peter 5:7] Cast all your cares upon Him and [Colossians 3:2] set your affections (mind) on things above, not on things on the earth.** Because the believer in Christ is in union with the new and face everyday challenges the King's perception for the chosen generation in all seasons is to think, say, vision and prescribe what KING JESUS has already mandated about your life and to see beyond the restrictions in those seasons. This will take sacrifice and discipline. The Kingdom of GOD -the mind of Christ- Governing Authority is never restricted… there are No restrictions in His divine sphere, even when one is disobedient or if one doesn't use God's power that's made available… by their own choice and unawareness a person put bars on their identity and destiny in Christ Jesus. People don't restrict the King or His Kingdom nor can anything in this sphere or the second heavens or heavens add to or subtract from GOD. No test… No temptation… No Sin… No title… No position… No threat… No law… No debate… No stubbornness… No lie… No devil can limit GOD! Think about that! The chain of limitations must be severed off of the mind. BREAK THE CHAIN! GOD moves on hearts of those who make the choice to trust, obey and do His will. Remember, Holy SPIRIT is the believer in Christ teacher and the revealer of the divine wisdom-thought-knowledge of GOD which authorizes us to defeat bondage, the devil's traps, break free and elevates our mind to another realm… the realm of the Lord's truth and freedom prosperity.

The scripture warns the believer in Christ about a wisdom that is earthly and is not from GOD; if a believer adheres to such wisdom of a corrupt nature frequency there will be a spiritual downslide. Jesus warns us to be on guard against the yeast [**Matthew 16:6**]. The teaching or values that redirect one's path to a wrong path or compromising path; whether in school, college, club groups and such like. A little leaven (sin) leavens (corrupts) the own lump. **The Bible tells us in [Jude 16, 19] These are murmurs, complainers walking after their own lusts; and their mouth speak great swelling words, having men's person admiration because of advantage. These be they who separate themselves, sensual and having not the Spirit.** Remember, carnal-minded souls do not comprehend the spiritual things of GOD, they're are hostile toward GOD and are tied to the sensual (senses-physical). **The Bible tells us in [Romans 8:5-8] For those who live according to the flesh set their minds on the things of the flesh, but those who live according to the Spirit, the things of the Spirit, For to be carnally mined is death, but to be spiritually minded is life and peace. Because the mind of the flesh**

is enmity against GOD: for it is not subject to the law of God; neither indeed can be. So then, those who are in the flesh cannot please God. Such attitudes and spirits are attracted to the carnal-mind because it can relate only to earthly-carnal wisdom; which is wisdom that can mislead and open the carnal-mind up to negativity, sinfulness and wickedness. This brings on bondage and perversion, such as twisting the Word of GOD. Believers in Christ are called out of darkness into the marvelous light to be a spiritual and holy people of GOD empowered to dominate the flesh. As children of GOD, we cannot be indulgers of men wisdom which is not wisdom from GOD above. This also includes seeking knowledge, answers, acceptance and solutions to health, relationships, financial issues or anything by means such as fortune tellers, psychics, readings, tarot cards or horoscopes, etc. which are outside results of inner spiritual decaying… satan is the source of such evils. It's diabolic and mental confinement… bondage. Earthly wisdom that is contrary to the plan and will of GOD will deter the soul from the eternal things of GOD. This should not be entertained within the new life of the believer in Christ. Such doors lead a soul into abdominal things, false worship and insensitivity to the Spirit of GOD. These things seek to rob souls of its birthright and imprison the mind. **The Bible tells us in [James 3:13a-15] Who is a wise man and endued with knowledge among you? Let him show by his good conduct that his deeds are done in gentleness of wisdom. But if ye have bitter, envying, jealousy, selfish ambition and strife in your hearts, boast not and don't lie against the Truth. This wisdom descended not from above, but is earthly, sensual and devilish.** These are worldly vices use to lure us away from GOD at anytime in any situation. Free people turn their back to slavery (sin's bondage) never to look to it again. Cast such non sense away. It seeks to control, manipulate, remove and strip a believer of their royal seat in Christ Jesus.

Wrong wisdom is wrong judgment, wrong discernment, wrong persuasion which leads to wrong thinking, wrong decision and wrong actions that can do internal and external damage… short or long term. It isn't what persuasion we hear, it's what we do with persuasions once it's heard. Little faith renders a soul doubtful uncertain and waverly because little faith is parallel to lack… little faith seeks for answers without truly trusting GOD; while action faith is persistent in knocking and seeking and asking GOD. Faith breaks chains and delivers promises. **The Bible tells us in [Mark 7:15] It's what comes out of a person that makes a person unclean or defiles him.** Believing hearts, we must ask Holy Spirit personally to teach us how to guard our hearts from falling into the lack of faith and against spiritual contamination. Persuasion consists of 1) authority 2) commitment 3) agreeable and 4) disagreeable. When you think of how persuasion works through self examination or observation these may very well surface. *Persuasion in the Hebrew means attempt to convince, argue, allure, instigate. Persuasion in the Greek means confidence, inward certainty, urgency. Wisdom in the Greek comes from the word Sophia which means divine, supernatural god-ordain intelligence, skill, godly insight and knowledge. Wisdom in the Hebrew comes from the word Chokmah which means the ability to see or discern the nature of something from God's view.* Earthly wisdom is not from GOD nor can it produce GOD supernatural value. Peter in his innocence called himself protecting Jesus from the prophesy of His death, but in **Matthew 16:23** Jesus turned and said to Peter, "Get behind me satan!" You are a stumbling block to me; you do not have in mind the things of God, but the things of men. We all can relate to our own wisdom and own understanding, but not consider if it's from GOD or from self… use this comparison to produce trust **[Proverbs 3:5]**. This too is measured by the plumb line, the Word of GOD. Every thought and intent which leads to actions come from your motives will be examined by GOD and His wisdom. Wrong wisdom can sound correct and innocent; yet, entrapment comes in many influential forms. This is sin pollution and entrapment in the soul from not living in faith. **The Bible tells us in [Proverbs 3:5] Trust in the Lord with all thine heart; and lean not to your own understanding. In all thy ways acknowledge the Lord and He will direct your paths.** Trust counteracts temptation, fear, sin and doubt entrapment. Entrapment, an undetected trap, is like being pushed into a corner with no way out. Entrapment can be discerned and uncovered by GOD in order for a believer to maneuver beyond limits. Such chains can be broken before it forms completely. Life choices have everything to do with the CROSS.

Once a thought is sown it performs like a seed; a seed is the carrier of thought, creativity and vision. The imagination can produce healthy or unhealthy emotional disturbances that can trigger the mind (feelings-thinking). Such thoughts and emotions that trigger wrong wisdom and wrong persuasion can only be dealt with through the finished work of the CROSS. That which is spiritually toxic is overcome by the Blood of Jesus, the Spirit and His Eternal Word. It's the darkness within that we must cast out and overcome... BREAK THE CHAIN! Remember, bondage doesn't discriminate, seize to retaliate or challenge because one believes in Christ. Circumstances that we create or that come our way directly or indirectly will lead one into making a choice. Circumstances that we had no say in or maybe happen before you where born or in your childhood can pass energies and stir up unwarranted feelings within the soul. And No, it's not fair. Christ was dealt unfairness, callousness, sabotage, resentment, lies and betrayal from his own people when he walked the earth; yet, Yeshua (Jesus) demonstrated to us what to do in such matters in order to overcome poison that rise from within to defile the soul and poison sown by others against you like Joseph's case... the persuasion of his brothers. This isn't the time to point fingers or find fault like Adam. This is the time to knock, pray and seek GOD, be strengthen in faith to press and push, seek your healing and deliverance in love and forgiveness regardless of who did or said what. This is the time to push to birth the promises of GOD. Your CONFIDENCE and LOVE For GOD must be GREATER than the disappointment, rejection, hurt, void, lies, abandonment and fear. This is a spiritual dosage we must apply daily. BE SET FREE! Break The Chain!

Many of us have found ourselves in pits similar to that of Joseph, the son of Jacob. Joseph pit revolved from within the family… family issues. Everybody's pit is different. Pits are associated with decay, death, depression, isolation and gloomy. The pit will affect one's attitude, faith level, feelings, behavior, character and future. The pit affects those led by the Spirit of GOD (Master), those led by the carnal nature (master), the lost and the backslider. The pit should not have the same affect when the believer humbly learns through it what GOD desires from it. The flesh mind will scream to the body to act out, get even, lose sight, etc, but those that thirst for GOD will cry out to GOD, seek His face and wait on Him. Seeking God's wisdom will turn the situation around to the work out for your good and God's good pleasure. The pits are there to teach the soul… the soul what it means to walk with GOD… to experience GOD… to grow in GOD… to trust GOD. The pits are also there to reveal the demonstrative power of GOD through the believer above the issue, to help the believer discovery his purpose and to walk in his/her spiritual gift(s). This revealing is literally a spiritual opening up of the soul to remove what doesn't belong, develop character, spiritual muscle and to deposit a measure of eternal revelation and wisdom. This is the Holy Spirit supernaturally filling the soul and activating spiritual Truth and blessings into the soul while putting carnality to death. That soul through any test, trial or tribulation now has access under the Spirit's direction to conquer in the realm of the spirit and see the manifestations of the promises of GOD. Triumphant Church we are like the Eagle; we watch in alertness with a keen spiritual eye, soar above the dross and conquer.

When the soul is in charge -carnality- it cannot understand spiritual things. Your heart-mind-soul has to become dependent, in harmony to the LORD. If not, the realm of the Holy Spirit is closed to that soul and that soul cannot understand. Eternal revelation, knowledge, wisdom and spiritual understanding come from the Spirit of GOD not the flesh -old man. Remember, the "I" (ego-pride-carnality) syndrome is commanded to be dethroned. **The Bible tells us in [1 Corinthians 2:14-15] But the natural (soulish, fleshly) man does not receive the things of the Spirit of GOD, for they are foolishness to him; nor can he know them, because they are spiritually discerned. But he who is spiritual judges all things, yet he himself is rightly judged by no one.** This has everything to do with the urgency of understanding the revelation of being set free in Christ... FREEDOM... because in pits the flesh tend to dictate and call the next move; when in reality the believer in Christ has been called and authorized to prophesy change, destiny while in the pit. It's the place of activation; yet dying to the mind of the flesh. It has nothing to do with the office of a prophet, but the spiritual gifts operating through the apostolic faith. Believers are commanded to speak what GOD has said about the situation; not complain or sit by silently or idle. We have to be WORD WALKERS! Pits that are there are to "Push" you into the next level for an anointing increase. Your life depends on the manifestation of the increase of GOD. Although our pits appear to be gloomy, it is the place for you and I to rise in dominion and power through our identity in Christ. The pit can be viewed as a spiritual and natural training camp for the soul to develop divine insight, be purged, spiritual maturity or the door to accepting salvation. The pit is just as much spiritual as it is natural. In many cases, a pit is also used to draw the heart-soul to GOD from its territory (location) for God's good will, pleasure and purpose. Remember, believers are to perform the King JESUS decree's while in such seasons. It's not a feeling of emotion; although pain and suffering exist, but it is an act of faith and obedience to

GOD. The Holy Spirit helps us to see when the soul is out of order or needs to move out of the way of GOD so GOD can have His way in us. The pit is there to teach you how to reach GOD, declare the WORD to the atmosphere and reveal to you who GOD called you to be. It's Kingdom!

The unrestrained lust within a heart wants to apprehend the reality of complete liberation against those that have confessed Christ Jesus as LORD and Savior. In times of trouble or pit experiences unrestrained lust within the heart wants to have its way… that leads to chaos. If we seek GOD patiently for total healing the reaction is different than seeking and giving up or not seeking at all. It's better to have GOD in your troubles than to be in trouble without know defense help. Freedom grace starts from the inside of the heart and mind never from the outside. Joseph learned the knowledge and divine revelation of this mystery through experience with the LORD through each pit; yet, his mind was not taken captive into slavery. He trusted GOD. The LORD was with him and he succeeded in spite of the resentment, betrayal, family denial, hatred, deep hurt, jealousy, rejection, loneliness and being sold into slavery **[Genesis 37 & 39]**. Looking from a carnal wisdom Joseph had every right to feel hostile and get revenge against all he came in contact with and lose hope because of what somebody else did to him. Emotions can erupt with corrosion from pitfalls: What some man or women did or didn't for you; division in a marriage or sexual identity crisis; dysfunctional family issues. Majority in the Church have experienced or are experiencing emotional pollution that brings entrapment. We don't expect or look or knowingly invite them, but such intruders will show up. The adversary plan is to ambush and kill the believer's destiny, but what is lodged in the spirit of the believer in Christ is greater than that which opposes believers. The Kingdom of GOD is within you for activation and demonstration **[Luke 17:20-21]**. Break The Chain!

The pits in a life can generate two spheres: sphere of light and the sphere of darkness. The darkness details all impurities within our character that tends to smother victory reality. The light details the illumination that brings forth victory in Christ Jesus. Light releases godly wisdom that I am not bound, but free in Jesus through the blood. The spirit of rejection is a demonic seed with a cord that will spread corruption to the mind and whole body. This spirit can open the door to same sex relationships, pornography, addictions, abomination cravings, over eating, selfish ambition, greed, manipulation or infidelity and such. This must be cast out and the cord severed in JESUS Name. Deep hurt often is released through the spirit of rejection's poisoned or brained washed persuasions that must be severed/ cut. When these doors remain open in the spirit realm things will begin to manifest openly from entertaining the forbidden... remember, the adversary don't come out of the box all at once he unfolds his agenda with the appearance of innocence like a treat in front of a child... CUT THE CORD IN JESUS NAME! A baby in Christ does not understand as those that are seasoned or mature in Christ. However, we all can ask for the wisdom of GOD in order to judge righteously, walk in complete deliverance and practice right from wrong. Unclean spirits seeks to keep a soul hostage from Truth which is the door to freedom. Because it is a spiritual matter, take authority in Yeshua's Name and command that thing(s) to be severed, broken by the authority of the Holy Spirit.

The spirit of rejection will open unseen doors linked to the spirit of fear, malice, no mercy, judgmental, anguish, retaliation, fabrication, rage, denial, perversion, idolatry and lies to build a fortress around what it justifies as being right for the protection of its territory; the mind-soul... CUT THE CORD IN YESHUA'S NAME! Poison, corrupt information, that a parent past on to their child(s) about the other parent can form a thought which creates an action can generate behavior from one generation to the next. It is the Blood of Yeshua HaMashiach (Jesus Christ) that breaks self-inflicted curses such as that and the Word that uproots the slander. SEVER THE CORD

And BREAK THE CHAIN! Remember, the darkness from within a soul is cast out by the Power of the Spirit, the Word and the Blood of the Lamb of GOD. It takes the Light to expel darkness from within the soul. **The Bible tells us in [Psalm 119:130] the Entrance of thy Word bringeth light and understanding to the simple.** The spirit of greed opens unseen wicked doors to the soul in the same manner as rejection, linked to with covetousness, lasciviousness (wanton, self indulgent), licentiousness (no moral restraints) and conforming to self rules. When a soul has conformed to this state of mind deliverance, godly counsel, renunciation, forgiveness, eternal salvation and a mind to choose new life in Christ is the antidote for freedom and healing. **The Bible tells us in [James 1:13-15] Let no man say when he is tempted, I am tempted of God: for God cannot be tempted with evil, neither tempt he any man: but every man is tempted, when he is drawn away of his <u>own</u> lust and enticed. Then when the lust hath conceived, it brings forth sin; and sin when it is finished brings forth death.** The Power of the CROSS decapitates the enemies of our souls. The Power of the CROSS destroys the conception of death and separation. The Power of the CROSS destroys sin process of habitually forming and functioning. The Word of GOD is the Light for our souls.

A worshipper and a warrior through the influence of Holy Spirit recognize the influence of the enemy of the state. Believers in Christ must become aware of satan's tactics and wisdom he uses to gain a foothold or an opportunity into the soul **[Ephesians 4:27]**. His information can pass through television shows, music, company, movies, games, entertainment or a conversation -devil's tongue- to charm a weak or baby Christian; matter of fact, anyone that lends an ear to his cunningness. The ear is a gate into your soul. The physical realm and spiritual realm has an ear. Therefore, as spiritual beings the Church must know the Word of GOD in order to speak the Word of GOD. Spiritual beings speak by the Spirit (Word) which is Spirit (Light) in the realm of the spirit. Light enters when Light is spoken. Speak Light! Believers in Christ Jesus have been given power and authority to overcome all the power of the enemy [**Luke 10:19**]. The believer have divine power to cast out demons and heal the sick [**Mark 3:15, 16:17; Matthew 10:8; Acts 26:18**]. Therefore, do not give unclean spirits any boundaries to sow or grow. Holy Spirit teaches and imparts to all born from above such wisdom and revelation from the Father. It's up to the born again to thirst, hunger, humble, indulge and receive Truth instructions. Since Christ is our stronghold -Strong Tower- no other hold should hold a faithful believing soul captive. JESUS breaks all false powers, false wisdom, false humility, false conversion and destroys ungodly soul-ties through salvation... grace... freedom. **The Bible tells us in [Psalm 9:9-10] The LORD is a refuge for the oppressed, a stronghold in times of trouble. Those who know your name trust in you, for you LORD, have never forsaken those who seek you.** The word stronghold which is parallel to refuge is used by the mighty, gifted worshipping warrior of GOD, King David. *Stronghold comes from the Hebrew word Ma'uzzi: a place of protection, safety, comfort and supply.* The refuge and stronghold is the LORD. Now is the time for you to speak... prophesy from the kingly position of authority in the power of the Holy Spirit and shut down the enemy's manipulation and persuasion... release the Kingdom of GOD. I charge you this day to give every unclean thought, unclean word, unclean association, unclean deed, image, vision and residue a Holy Spirit eviction. No notice is required only the Command of Holy Spirit and Holy Spirit is already ready to press forward the Father's will. When a soul runs into and takes hold of that STRONGHOLD... GOD provision of supply is rewarded. Portions of that supply in this fortified place are Healing, Love, Acceptance, Transformation, Wholeness, Restoration, Increase, True Identity and Empowerment for the inner man. We must activate this Truth in all times... a constant sowing of the Word of GOD. Forgiven grace terminates wickedness. We overcome with increasing faithfulness to GOD.

It's Not From God...
Command it to Break!

Father GOD, In the Name Of Jesus, You Said Every Knee Shall Bow At Your Name And I'm Taking You At Your Word. I Command Every Evil Spirit To Break In Jesus Name By The Authority of The Holy Spirit... Loose The People Of GOD! Let Them Go In Jesus Name!

UNBELIEF BREAK! DOUBT BREAK! FEAR BREAK! WHOREDOM BREAK! CALLOUS HEART BREAK! RETALIATION BREAK! PREJUDICE BREAK! LOVE FOR THE WORLD BREAK! LOVE OF MONEY BREAK! DRUG DEPENDENCY BREAK! REJECTION BREAK! SMOKING, NICOTINE BREAK! LOW SELF ESTEEM BREAK! STRIFE BREAK! HYPROCRISY BREAK! RELIGIOUS DEMON BREAK! UNGODLY PATTERNS BREAK! ANXIOUSNESS BREAK! FAMILIAR SPIRITS BREAK! COMPROMISE BREAK! PROCRASTINATION BREAK! EGO BREAK! DENIAL BREAK! MURMURRING BREAK! COMPLAINING! LUST SPIRIT BREAK! SEDUCTION BREAK! PORNO-SPIRIT BREAK! TORMENTING SPIRIT BREAK! RAGE BREAK! MALICE! COVETOUSNESS BREAK! THE LORD REBUKES YOU! LOOSE YOUR HOLD IN JESUS NAME!

FREEDOM SCRIPTURE STUDY

PSALM 34:14

Turn from evil and do good; seek peace and pursue it.

PSALM 29: 11

The LORD gives strength to his people; the
LORD blesses his people with peace.

PROVERBS 12:20

Deceit is in the heart of those who plot evil,
but those who promote peace have joy.

ACTS 3:19

Repent, then, and turn to God, so that your sins may be wiped
out, that times of refreshing may come from the Lord.

PSALM 51:1-3; 7

Have mercy upon me, O God, according to your loving kindness;
according to the multitude of your tender mercies, blot out my
transgressions, wash me thoroughly from my iniquities and
cleanse me from my sin. For I acknowledge my transgression
and my sin is ever before me. Purge me with hyssop and I
shall be clean, wash me and I shall be whiter than snow.

PSALM 86:5

For thou, Lord, art good, and ready to forgive;
and plenteous in mercy unto all them that
call upon thee.

LUKE 6:37b

Forgive and you shall be forgiven.

REVELATION 1:5

... and from Jesus Christ, the faithful witness, the firstborn
of the dead and the ruler of the kings of the earth to Him
who loves us and released us from sins by His blood.

JOHN 8:36

So if the Son sets you free, you will be free indeed.

1 PETER 2:16

Live as free people, but do not use your freedom as a cover-up
for evil; but use it and live as bondservants of God.

2 PETER 2:9

... then the Lord knows how to rescue the godly
from temptation and to keep the unrighteous
under punishment for the Day of Judgment.

2 CORINTHIANS 3:17

Now the Lord is the Spirit and where the
Spirit of the Lord is, there is freedom.

1 CORINTHIANS 6:12

I have the right to do anything, you say, but not
everything is beneficial. I have the right to do
anything, but I will not be mastered by anything.

GALATIANS 3:22

But scripture has locked up everything under the control of
sin, so that what was promised, being given through faith
in Jesus Christ, might be given to those who believe.

GALATIANS 5:1

It is for freedom that Christ has set us free. Stand firm, then and
do not let yourselves be burdened again by the yoke of bondage.

GALATIANS 5:13-14

You, my brothers and sisters, were called to be free. But do
not use your freedom to indulge the flesh; rather, serve one
another humbly in love. For the entire law id fulfilled in
keeping this one command, love your neighbor as yourself.

ROMANS 6:22

But now that you have been set free from sin and
have become slaves of GOD, the benefit you reap
leads to holiness and the result is eternal life.

PSALM 118:5

When hard pressed, I cried to the LORD;
he bought me into a spacious place.

PSALM 119:45

I will walk about in freedom, for I have sought out your precepts.

EPHESIANS 3:12

In him and through faith in him we may approach
God with freedom and confidence.

EPHESIANS 5:27

… that He might present to Himself the church in
all her glory, having no spot or wrinkle or any such
thing; but that she would be holy and blameless.

1 THESSALONIANS 5:23

Now may the God of peace Himself sanctify you entirely;
and may your spirit and soul and body be preserved complete,
without blame at the coming or our Lord Jesus Christ.

Greek word for Offense

Skandalon: to trap, trip up, stumbling block, strike against, to do harm to

Greek word for Repent

Metanoia: (repentance) change one's mind or purpose for a better course of life, change in the inner man

Greek words for Forgive

Aphesis: to send away, dismiss, release, let go, pardon and deliverance

Charizomai: the act of exercising grace from the heart outwardly toward one who may be guilty in spite of the crime done against another, show kindness, favor

Hebrew word for Forgive

Salach: to pardon (authorized by God)

Divine forgiveness perfect transforming rule is performed through humility, faith and obedience. What is important to the believer is the divine wisdom to live out the principle of forgiveness when it's challenged, how to unleash the expression of freedom through Christ to break barriers and how to walk in freedom in spite of what is happening or what happened... Power of the CROSS. Yes, we know it's available, but to see the power manifest in our soul is necessary for the outcome of true change. Having an understanding of divine forgiveness work is to think it, see it and walk it. Vision yourself wearing it like a second skin... you see the picture... cloaked in the agape of Jesus from within; the anointing to demonstrate the way from within. God's divine grace makes you different by His nature. GOD never said it was easy, but said by obedience men will, not should, will know that you are my disciples. Although many minds are familiar with being forgiven many struggle inwardly with forgiveness nature and the ability to relate it to others, as well as, to self. Because salvation is the free gift wrapped in divine forgiveness, the blood sacrifice, to perform an act of divine love and discipline calls for dependence on the Ruach Hakodesh (Holy Spirit) to demonstrate this grace substance in our lives as situations come and go... fruitfulness is substance of its seed and source. **The Bible tells us in [Matthew 3:8] Produce fruit in keeping repentance... prove by the way you live that you have repented of your sins and turned to God.** The seed of righteousness (Christ) produces fruitfulness through the Power of the Holy Spirit... a continual work for the spiritual building... the new soul. Holy Spirit imputes righteousness by faith **[John 9:31]**.

Jesus (Yeshua) demonstrated the way "in Christ" how we are to humble and follow at the cost of surrendering our will as being a new creature in Him. It's a daily crucifying of the carnal mind (mind of the flesh) the applying the Word of GOD to put on Christ. Just as it was agony for Christ it will be exhausting in our own strength and own mind to walk in this realm. Its takes a willing heart to abide in faith, ready to let it go of it all, deny yourself, take up your cross and follow Christ. Christ is the head that leads His body accordingly by faith and obedience and love. Believers in Christ Jesus have nothing to lose, but much to gain. It may appear that you have something to lose, but in reality flesh is decaying. The inner man will rebound through the Spirit of GOD and mature spiritually and naturally. ABBA sees His Church through His Son and has already made provision for the body of Christ to come out on top in heart and deed through obedience. In return what has been given unto us is expected to be given out removing the offense as it cost Christ to do. Christ made the ultimate sacrifice of giving up Himself for all souls; therefore, we are commanded to follow His example and instructions. There may be consequences to be resolved in the physically due to behavior, but the crime is erased from that heart's spiritual account by GOD until that soul repeats the incriminating acts over again… which calls for repentance. Receiving forgiveness grace act into the heart cancels out the indictment and vengeance that souls deserve from GOD. It destroys the contract of alienation, being an enemy of GOD. It destroys the contract from the father of lies, satan. Forgiveness breaks every chain and cord that's in violation of the CROSS and scatters His enemies which are also the body of Christ enemies by His Holy Fire… one of the functions of the Holy Spirit… in both the spiritual and physical realms.

The adversary from the beginning has always twisted Truth to make the twist appealing to the flesh -carnal mindset- that it's okay. In satan's craftiness he convinces the soul that God's instructions or promises aren't what you think they mean. The father of lies twists God's realities with an apparition (vision, image) destine to gain control and doorway into any soul that falls to the liar lies. The devil, as a roaring lion, seeks whom he may devour. He seeks for open minds and hearts for access into the soul and will make it seem like its innocent; due to the emotions. The enemy will play on emotions and thoughts to imprison us from within. Remember, as I stated in another section, our emotions can be corrupt as well… emotions are to come into alignment by submitting to the Word of GOD. **The Bible tells us in [2 Corinthians 10:5] Casting down imaginations and every high thing that exalt itself against the knowledge of God and bringing into captivity every thought to the obedience of Christ.** GOD thought revealed -His Logos- the Word, cautions us about the sphere of the mind; showing us that that's a spiritual domain that can shape impure thoughts leading to unjust actions and/ or behavior *(Purchase: Bloodline Spiritual DNA)*. Whatever is conceived in the mind will give birth or delivery in the natural sphere. **The Bible tells us in [Proverbs 23:7] For as he think in his heart so is he.** All that we are in Christ is measured by the Word of GOD, not feelings or opinions that aren't tempered by the Fire of GOD. Remember, the CROSS has taken everything into consideration for victory to abound. The believer's inborn essence, vision, identity, character, royalty, future, authority, power and persuasion is signed, sealed and delivered only through the Blood of Christ… it speaks today because He's alive. And because the blood speaks life you are to declare wholeness of thought, imagination, mind, temperance (self control), long life and divine order to occupy your will and life.

We think that forgiveness comes automatic with no hindrances or withdrawal symptoms, but in many cases it's not that simple; yet, possible. When a person has been misused, verberally or physically abused, made to feel like nothing, mistreated, abandon, rejected, cheated on or such like, although we know we are to forgive, forgiveness does not rise to the top of the thought list, but rather other feelings seem to make there arrival known. Scars of the heart do not heal or go away so easily or are easily forgotten. Such opened wounds that are not healed pierces like fragmented glass in the soul. It cuts to the core forming spiritual chains and spiritual bleeding of the soul. These chain links will build a secure place in the heart to safeguard against anything that appears as a threat to that soul. The choice not to forgive brings one under condemnation and denial... demonic contamination. Forgiveness requires the sacrifice of self. Repeat: FORGIVENESS REQUIRES THE SACRIFICE OF MYSELF! This hurts the flesh feelings, control and pride, but GOD is love and His love is without measure. He commands us to forgive without record... unlimited times unlimited and love without measure. This calls for SUBMISSION with much prayer. This is supernatural and will demand the dying of the old nature's mindset. **Peter came to Yeshua and asked a stimulating question: Lord how many times or how often should I forgive my brother who commits an offense (sin) against me? Seven times? Yeshua (Jesus) said not seven times, but seventy-seven times [Matthew 18:21-22].** God's mercy always rejoices against judgment. Break The Chain!

As GOD opens the soul up it's the Law of Christ that saturates and plows the heart. The plowing can be painful, but in the end it reaps a harvest of eternal peace, love, harmony and favor. The Word of GOD is seed. It is the authority to terminate or produce. No matter what you hold against yourself, what somebody does or has done to you, there is strength, healing, grace and truth available through Ruach Hakodesh (Holy Spirit) for you to walk in forgiveness with no strings attached; and power to pray for those who despitefully use you **[Matthew 5:44-48]**. Praying for our enemies in unconditional love sincerely releases a supernatural exchange of healing into our soul. GOD GRACE IS SUFFICIENT AND HIS STRENGTH IS MADE PERFECT IN WEAKNESS **[2 Corinthians 12:9]**. The New Covenant is freedom from all unauthorized restraints, patterns, nets, hooks and chains that seek to keep a soul locked up in the mind; shutdown darkness through your liberty in Christ. Believers are called to be the temple of GOD… the dwelling place of the Holy Spirit.

Walking in forgiveness toward others is the law of the Kingdom of Yahweh. Caution: if you do not forgive others of their offenses against you, ABBA will not forgive you of your sins; offenses against His justice. Offense is another term for sin and being offended is the result of an offense. Hearts are in violation of the CROSS that holds someone in prison because one has been offended by someone else's actions in word, deed, looks or behavior. Such a violation causes for purging by the Word and the Blood of Yeshua. JESUS has provided provision for souls to overcome the spiritual attack of offense. But that soul personally must be willing to partake of the forgiven grace provided in order to obtain victory in the face of offenses. The spirit of denial and rejection works within bitter emotional feelings of regret, resentment, anguish and pride. You don't want to stand before the LORD who is holy with unlawful violations (spots) in the heart reflecting darkness instead of light when He has made healing available for you. **The Bible tells us in [Hebrews 4:12' For the word of God is alive. Sharper than any double-edged sword, it penetrates even to dividing soul and spirit, joints and marrows; it judges the thoughts and attitudes of the heart. Nothing of all creation is hidden from God's sight. Everything is uncovered and laid bare before the eyes of him to whom we must give account.** Yahweh must see the Blood Stain Banner of Yeshua sprinkled in the heart, not see your flesh; which will unveil the wrath of GOD toward rebellious souls that stubbornly don't consider their ways and repent. **The Bible tells us in [Haggai 1:5] Now therefore, saith the Lord of hosts, Consider thy ways.** That is a spiritual warning to all followed by consequences.

Unclean spirits may gain a legal entry into a believer's life through past sins that aren't confessed or through generational patterns (bloodline) rooted in unconfessed sins through spiritual gateways. Through a believer's spiritual gates (eyes, ears) which sin may have entered and are not confessed (not placed under the blood) gives the devil legally right to enter until those gateways are closed by way of repentance and forgiving. That illegal right of entrance is broken under the New Covenant through the BLOOD of YESHUA, rendered non-effective… stamped CANCELED! When a soul is not saved they are under the authority and dominion of satan, but when a soul is in the Lord they are no longer under that dominion (rule) or authority (power) of satan. Therefore, the devil has no authority or power over the believer unless one is living in habitually sinning which opens doorways for the adversary. When GOD declared He will bless you for obedience and curse you for disobedience He was talking to His covenant people; not to those that were not in covenant with Him **[Leviticus 26]. The Bible tells us in [Matthew 4:4] Man shall not live by bread alone, but by every word that proceed out of the mouth of GOD.** Recognize, identify, break contracts and close the gate(s) in Yeshua's powerful name by the power of His Word. Forgiveness renders all past offense charges void. Forgiveness acceptance cancels the charge against and holds no record of offense or sin. This sacrificial act of grace transfers the soul to the state of mercy found in love… guilt erased. The only person that can continue to bring it up is the individual that chooses to return back to their vomit and rehearse it. And refuses not to let go the offense done to them or they've done to others or others used by the devil to hold them in their past. The past does not exist in our present or future. The past is the old way of life with its adulterated deeds left in the past… behind you. What is behind you is not permitted to lead or dictate to you. There is no past in forgiven grace. It Is Finished! You live in the future present… FREEDOM… new life hidden in Christ. This is your authorization and freedom right through the Blood of Jesus.

Feeling of resentment like hatred comes through an offense. This is spiritual slavery and confinement. A seed of offense is sown before the very act is committed. An offense is defined as a scandal, evil set up waiting to grip any available mind and soul. Yahweh is holy and just, nothing profane can stand expecting grace without humbly receiving His forgiveness through the CROSS to restore the spiritual state according to the His law. Who are we not to release others and not let go the bitterness caused by pain. An unforgiving heart condition is not a blessing. Though pain can hurt deeply it is the place to personally experience who GOD say He is to you. Faith, humility, commitment and obedience are keys to a constant victory. **The Bible tells us in [Romans 14:23]... everything that does not come from faith is sin.** What is not of faith is motivated by death and not life. Holding grudges is a freedom blocker and blessing blocker. Because its seed creates bondage; it binds, blocks maturity, blocks promotion, blocks the manifestations of the Kingdom of GOD, stunts to kill spiritual growth, demotes and hinders your destiny. Unforgiveness will blackout emotions that where not created to be cold. GOD who is holy and compassionate will not move outside of His justice to accommodate injustice. The LORD requires a heart knowledge experience which displays a fruitful action in thought and behavior out of a clean heart. He is the physician, surgeon for the heart and the advocate for our believer's soul. All that does not apply to the believer must be dealt with on this side by the cutting away of all that resists the Blood of the Lamb of GOD. Our lawyer and defender Jesus tells us what the justice system of GOD the Father requires of us. And gives the willing believer all power to accomplish and walk upright in victory. Jesus as our lawyer and defender search the whole heart and have already set full bail through His WORD for ones' heart to transformation.

Forgiveness rooted in agape is a healer to the mind and the heart which brings healthiness and harmony to the body and to relationships far or near. Forgiveness reconciles family members, friends, removes pollution out of the heart and mends brokenness. Just as the power of forgiveness removes the hostility barrier between GOD and us; the same forgiven grace works for us when we truly forgive those that we feel have wronged us. The LORD knows it can be achieved through His Power-Grace working effectively in the heart of those who will lean on Him for this favor to become a manifested reality within the heart, mind and soul. The Power of the CROSS concerns your total being. Love and forgiveness works unified to promote His Kingdom in the earth as one body, one spirit, one head and one mind. You cannot truly love your enemy without forgiving them and you cannot forgive your enemies without truly loving GOD. It is impossible because Jesus life, talk and walk demonstrated the love of ABBA for wrenched mankind; yet, despising all the shame He endured the CROSS. This agape is not an emotional roller caster type of love, its an activated action from being in union with GOD. Love and forgiveness work hand in hand. **The Bible tells us in [John 13:35] by this all men shall know that you are the Lord's disciples that you have love (unconditional, kingdom) toward one another.** Forgiveness is a never ending attitude in the life of a true Christian who fears of the LORD and dwells in the secret place of the Most High. When we are walking in forgiveness it shows obedience, the love of GOD in the heart of those that fear Him and submission to GOD; dying to the flesh nature and growing from faith to faith.

Forgiveness is fruitful and unforgiving is unfruitful. They both bare seed of its nature. One fruit is sweet and can speak wholeness the other fruit is wicked with bitterness springing forth from its core. If a good seed or bad seed is sown, you will get a return on what was planted. GOD is Just. He looks at the heart of man and judges according to our deeds which are driven by the motives of the heart. The LORD is the righteous judge. He judges all according to His holy justice. I encourage you to examine and search your heart and measure it not by the offense, pain or hurt, but by the Power of the finished work of the CROSS and the Eternal Word. Jesus shows us our character and shows us the cleansing power through the grace of forgiveness that sets us free. This is a glorious walk in a person's life, making the step forward, putting bondage in the grave and severing the cords that bind; that's deliverance and liberation for the soul. Break the chain by choosing to be free through the Power of the CROSS. JESUS, our liberator, liberates the body, soul, mind and heart releasing a measure of eternity's equity and benefits.

PERSONAL NOTES

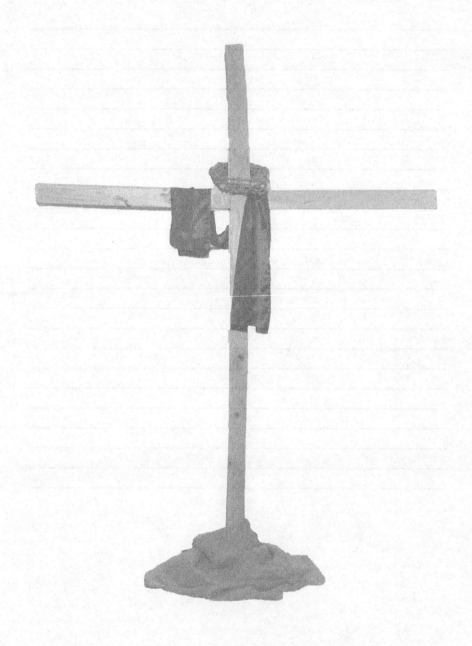

FAITH CONFESSION PRAYER

Heavenly Father, in the Name that is above every name, Jesus Christ, I come before your Throne of Grace and Mercy asking you to cleanse all defilement that you see in my heart. I confess I have been walking in _____, _____, _____, _____, doubt, hesitation, dishonesty, jealousy, bitterness, pay back, faultfinding, procrastination, manipulation, deceit, idleness, prayerlessness and/ or compromise; I repent right now whole heartily. I ask for your forgiveness in Jesus Name. Lord I pray for strength and increase in my relationship with you and with others. I pray that you teach me all things pertaining to godliness. Heavenly Father, I seek your face, infuse me with genuine humility, divine revelation, knowledge, counsel, love on the inward parts and godly wisdom. Fill me Lord with your Holy Spirit, increase my faith and overshadow me with the anointing to overcome my trials and tribulations, producing divine fruitfulness in my life. I die daily to my will that your will be done through me. Live through me Lord. Reveal your divine purpose for my life hidden in you. Lord, I humble myself under your hand, because I am powerless in my strength to combat this. I trust that you will exalt and establish me in due season in the Name of Jesus Christ. Increase supernaturally endurance and stability. Sanctify my heart, eyes, ears, tongue, attitude, behavior, emotions, life style and condition me Lord to handle what may come. Restore my family, finances, job, health, children, mind, prayer life and cause me to flourish in your holy Word in Jesus Name.

Amen.

DELIVERANCE PRAYERS:

I DECREE THE POWER OF FORGIVENESS TO FLOOD MY SPIRIT, HEARTS, THOUGHTS, ACTIONS AND IMAGINATION NOW IN JESUS NAME. BY THE AUTHORITY OF HOLY SPIRIT I SPEAK HEALING TO MY SOUL AND COMMAND MY SPIRIT MAN TO RISE IN JESUS NAME. I COMMAND MY THOUGHTS, HEART, BEHAVIOR AND SPEECH TO COME INTO HOLY ALIGNMENT WITH THE WORD OF GOD IN JESUS NAME.

IN THE NAME OF JESUS BY THE AUTHORITY OF HOLY SPIRIT, I DENOUNCE ALL UNCLEAN SPIRITS AND RELENTLESS ACTS, DOUBT, ANGER, LASCIVIOUSNESS, REJECTION, IDENTITY CRISIS, RACISM, BITTERNESS, RAGE, COLDHEARTEDNESS, MEAN SPIRIT, CONTROL, FAULTFINDING, DOUDLE MINDEDNESS, HYPROCRISY AND HOLDING GRUDGES BE GONE FROM MY DWELLING IN THE NAME OF JESUS CHRIST. I COMMAND THE CORDS, BONDS AND UNLAWFUL SOUL TIES TO BE SEVERED IN JESUS NAME. I COMMAND EVERY DOOR THAT HOLDS ME TO MY PAST TO CLOSE IN JESUS NAME. I TURN MY BACK TO MY PAST AND MY HEART AND FACE TO GOD.

I TAKE DIVINE AUTHORITY IN JESUS NAME THIS DAY. I BIND EVERY WHISPER, EVIL PERSUASION, VOICE AND EVERY DIABOLIC DEVISED PLAN SAID IN SECRET AGAINST ME. LORD SEND YOUR HOLY FIRE TO CONSUME, BRING DOWN ALL THE HIGH PLACES AND CHAINS THAT SOLICIT ME FOR DESTRUCTION IN JESUS NAME. I BIND THEIR ASSIGNMENTS AND THE WORD OF GOD SHATTERS THEIR PLANS. I COMMAND ALL PLANS BE THROWN INTO CONTINUAL CONFUSION. I APPLY THE BLOOD OF JESUS OVER THE DWELLING OF MY HOME, MY BODY, MY IMAGINATION, MY THOUGHTS, MY TONGUE, MY EMOTIONS, MY LIFE, MY

SPIRIT AND ALL THAT PERTAINS AND IS CONNECTED TO ME IN JESUS NAME.

I COMMAND MY SOUL, MY EMOTIONS, MY THOUGHTS, MY MIND, MY BODY AND ATMOSPHERE TO RESPOND TO THE WORD OF GOD. NO WEAPON FORMED AGAINST ME SHALL PROSPER IN JESUS NAME. LORD, I GIVE YOU THANKS, PRAISE AND WORSHIP FOR YOUR GLORY. YOUR WORD DOES NOT RETURN UNTO YOU VOID BUT ACCOMPLISHES WHEREFORTH IT HAS BEEN SENT ON MY BEHALF. YOUR WORD OH LORD IS ABSOLUTE, ETERNAL AND FOREVER SETTLED IN HEAVEN. YOU ARE NOT A MAN THAT YOU SHALL LIE. YOU HASTEN TO PERFORM YOUR WORD FOR THOSE WHO TRUST IN YOU. LORD I TRUST AND TAKE REFUGE IN YOU. THEREFORE, GATES OF HELL YOU SHALL NOT PREVAIL. IT'S SEALED AND FINISHED IN THE BLOOD OF JESUS.

WARFARE PRAYERS:

I TAKE AUTHORITY BY THE POWER AND AUTHORITY OF YAHWEH THAT EVERY CHAIN BE BROKEN OFF MY MIND, MY EMOTIONS, OFF MY CHILDRENS' MIND, FUTURE AND THERE CHILDREN. I COMMAND UNFRUITFUL SEEDS TO DRY UP AND DIE. I COMMAND EVERY IDLE, UNWHOLESOME WORD THAT HAS BEEN SPOKEN ABOUT ME OR TOWARD ME OR BY ME TO BE UPROOTED, FALL TO THE GROUND AND DIE. LORD, SEND YOUR HOLY FIRE INTO THE ATMOSHERE. EVERY EVIL YOKE OF THE DEVIL BE DESTROYED BY THE FIRE OF GOD IN THE NAME OF JESUS. BREATHE FRESH WIND HOLY SPIRIT.

FATHER IN THE NAME OF JESUS I RELEASE YOUR HOLY FIRE AGAINST THE SPIRIT OF OFFENSE, UNFORGIVENESS, RETAILATION, RESENTMENT, VEXES, BEWITCHMENT, VOODOO, BLACK MAGIC, BLOOD PACT INITIATIONS, CURSES, ALL SELF INFLICTED CURSES, ALL DEMONIC THOUGHTS, ASSIGNMENTS AND IDENTITY THEFT. HOLY SPIRIT COMSUME ALL THE RESIDUE OF MY PAST BY YOUR HOLY FIRE IN THE NAME OF JESUS. I COMMAND MY SOUL TO BE LOOSED FROM EVERY UNGODLY SOUL TIE... BREAK! BY THE AUTHORITY OF THE HOLY GHOST I COMMAND THE CHAINS TO BREAK! EVERY ACT OF PERVERSION, BREAK IN JESUS NAME! BREATHE FRESH WIND HOLY SPIRIT.

I BIND ALL DEMONIC THREAT, SPIRITUAL ATTACK AND TAKE THESE THINGS INTO CAPITIVITY IN YESHUA'S NAME BY FAITH... EVERY ILL SPOKEN WORD, WHISPER, CHANT, CURSE SPOKEN, TEXTED, WRITTEN OR FORMED DIRECTLY AGAINST MARRIAGE UNION, FAMILY MEMBERS, SPOUSES, FINANCES, SEX, INTIMACY, EDUCATION, VISION, MINISTRY, CHURCH, SEX IDENTITY CONFUSION, ADHD

ABNORMALITY, WELFARE, INCOME, BUSINESS, JOBS, PRENANCY, HAIR GROWTH, EYE VISION LOSS, HEALTH, BODY AND JOINT PAIN. I DECREE SUPERNATURAL DIVINE HEALING TO MANIFEST BY THE FIRE OF GOD. BREATHE FRESH WIND HOLY SPIRIT.

I DECREE DEBT CANCELATION, VOID (_____, _____), CURSED AT THE ROOT, BROKEN OFF AND DESTROYED OFF THE BLOODLINE AND RENDER ITS SEED SPOILIED, CAST DOWN AND THE SUPPLY LINE AND ALL REINFORCEMENTS PARALIZED SPIRITUALLY AND NATURALLY IN JESUS NAME. BREATHE FRESH WIND HOLY SPIRIT.

Our redeemer lives and because Jesus Lives, He lives within the believer and governs through the power of His Holy Spirit; being in Christ places believers in covenant bond with the Father... ABBA, Daddy, Yahweh. Therefore, decree His law concerning you by faith in the power and authority of the Ruach Hakodesh (Holy Spirit) daily. By faith speak life which Yeshua HaMashiach has already accomplished on the CROSS at Calvary. Decree and declare in faith, obedience and love daily by the authority and power of Holy Spirit. Listed next are 39 faith decree declarations representing the 39 stripes Jesus took willingly for our healing. Remember, believers in Christ are positioned to grow from faith to faith, glory to glory by the Spirit of Truth in submission.

KING JESUS DECREED IT TO BE SO

I DECREE THE WISDOM OF THE LORD BE ENLARGED IN MY CHILDRENS' HEART AND THE BLESSINGS OF THE LORD ENLARGE THEIR TERRITORY!

I DECREE THAT MY SEED AND CHILDREN SEED WALK, LIFE AND WILL BE IN ALIGNMENT WITH ABBA'S WILL!

I DECREE EVERY PLOT OF THE ENEMY AGAINST THE COUNTRY, LAWS OF THE LAND AND NATIONALITIES BE THROWN INTO DISARRAY!

I DECREE HOLINESS BE MANIFESTED IN MY INWARD PARTS BY THE POWER OF YOUR FIRE LORD!

I DECREE EVERY OBSTACLE BE OVERTURNED FOR MY GOOD AND FAITH BE INCREASED!

I DECREE THE DARKNESS FROM WITHIN BE SHATTER BY THE FIRE AND LIGHT OF GOD'S WORD!

I DECREE THE ANOINTING OF THE LORD REST ON ME!

I DECREE MY SOUL RESPOND TO THE LIGHT... THE WORD OF GOD!

I DECREE THAT EVERY IMPURE PERSUASION OF THE MIND BE BROUGHT DOWN LOW!

I DECREE THAT EVERY TRAP, SNARE, SET UP SENT TO ENTANGLE ME BE OVERTHROWN BY THE POWER OF GOD'S WORD AND HIS FIRE!

I DECREE THAT MY MIND AND HEART RESPOND WITH READINESS TO THE WILL OF THE FATHER!

I DECREE SOULS BE QUICKEN, MADE ALIVE, BY THE POWER AND FIRE OF GOD!

I DECREE MY FAMILY, FINANCES, HEALTH, VISION, FOCUS AND FAITH RECIEVE FLOODED BLESSINGS THROUGH COVENANT WITH GOD!

I DECREE THAT THE PEACE OF GOD THAT SURPASSES ALL UNDERSTANDING FLOOD MY HOME, THOUGHTS, EMOTIONS AND ATMOSPHERE!

I DECREE THAT FINANCAL RESOURCES LOCATE ME!

I DECREE DEBT CANCELLATION... GUILT AND SHAME, BE GONE FROM MY FAMILY LINE!

I DECREE THE SPIRIT OF CONTENTMENT FLOOD MY SOUL!

I DECREE THAT I'M ANXIOUS FOR NOTHING AND THE FRUIT OF THE SPIRIT INCREASE WITHIN ME!

I DECREE THE BLESSINGS OF THE LORD OVERSHADOW ME!

I DECREE THAT GODLY WISDOM, DESIRES, THOUGHTS AND PLANS BUILD MY LIFE!

I DECREE THAT I WALK IN THE BOUNDLESS RICHES OF THE LORD!

I DECREE THE FEAR OF THE LORD LOCATE THE HEARTS OF THE LOST, BACKSLIDER AND SATURATE HIS CHURCH!

I DECREE THAT EVERY NEED THAT CONCERNS MY HOUSEHOLD IS MET, HEALED, RESTORED AND MANIFESTED!

I DECREE BLESSINGS OF GRACE-FAVOR BE RELEASED OVER MY CHILDREN, GRANDCHILDREN, EDUCATION, JOB AND CAREER!

I DECREE DIVINE CONNECTIONS, DIVINE DOORS, DIVINE APPOINTMENTS, DIVINE INFLUENCE BE MANIFESTED!

I DECREE FAITH, UNDERSTANDING AND KNOWLEDGE TO INCREASE AND EXPAND IN ME!

I DECREE SPIRITUAL BLESSINGS OF LORD TO FILL ME!

I DECREE MY MIND BOW TO YESHUA (JESUS) AND THE MIND OF CHRIST BE ESTABLISHED!

I DECREE THAT ALL THAT CONCERNS ME IS MADE WHOLE; SPIRIT, MIND AND BODY!

I DECREE THAT EVERY GOOD THING FROM THE LORD BE ESTABLISHED AND MANFESTED TOWARD MY SEED!

I DECREE SUPERNATURAL TRANSFORMATION TO BE MANIFESTED IN MY SOUL!

I DECREE THE EYES OF MY UNDERSTANDING AND AN EAR TO HEAR THE LORD BE OPENED!

I DECREE MY STEPS, UPRISING AND DOWN-SITTING BE ORDERED BY THE SPIRIT OF THE LORD!

I DECREE I SHALL NOT FAINT, BUT SOAR IN THE SPIRIT BY THE POWER OF GOD!

I DECREE MY WAY IS MADE SUCCESSFUL THROUGH THE MEDITATION ON THE WORD OF GOD DAY IN DAY OUT!

I DECREE THE CROWN OF THE SPIRIT OF REVELATION, WISDOM, COUNSEL, KNOWLEGDE, UNDERSTANDING AND THE SPIRIT OF GOD REST UPON ME!

I DECREE SOULS! SOULS! SOULS NEAR AND FAR BE COMPEL TO HEAR, COME TO CHRIST AND THAT HIS OIL PERMEATE THEIR LIVES!

I DECREE THE PROSPERITY BENEFITS AND THE JUSTICE OF THE LORD MANIFEST IN THE CHURCH!

CONCLUSION

Beloved of GOD, guard your heart and let the Word of Christ dwell in you richly; whom the Son sets free is free indeed, no more bondage, for the Lord has delivered me. I'm Free in Christ by the Power of the Blood! I Walk Free! Talk Free! My Heart, Mind, Soul And Body Is Free! I Choose To Be Free In Christ! Declare it until it manifests.

GLOSSARY

Adonai: (Hebraic-pronounced ad ho nay) Hebrew title for God and his position, signifying sovereignty, Lord, LORD, Master

Adversary: foe, antagonist, enemy

Affections: inward parts, to set the mind on, depraved passions not guided by God, passions, lust, strong emotions

Apostasy: abandonment from previous loyalty and faith, a falling away, withdrawal

Atonement: to cover

Atonement of Christ: exchanging his righteousness for our guilt, restoration to favor, reconciliation through his blood; pardoning of sin

Bruise: crush, pain inflicted in the flesh, contrite

Commission: acts of sin in thought, word or deed; unintentional or intentional sin, sin acts committed

Covenant: a contract, agreement between God and his people

Covet: thirst after, itch after, lust after, to desire wrongfully

Decree: judgment, principle of God, royal order

Diabolic: satanic, unholy, wicked, evil, hellish, demonic

Equity: impartiality, justness, holy justice

Favor: to bend or stoop in mercy to another that is lesser in superiority, grace

Flog: victim strapped to a pole, to whip, beat, smite, severe pain, chastise

Forgiven: pardon, set free, to let go, discharge, liberate, to send away

Fruitful: profitable, to bear, to increase, grow

Grace: divine influence upon the heart, extension into action, favor

Holy: of God, sacredness, set apart from worldliness and darkness unto God in Christ by the Holy Spirit for his pleasure and purpose in the earth

Idolatry: giving recognition, worship, affirmation, bowing to, seeking of acceptance and sacrificing to anything as a god other than the one true God

Iniquity: disobedience, sin, wickedness, lawlessness

Longsuffering: steadfastness, patience, forbearance, slowness in avenging wrongs

Lordship: to rule or govern by the Spirit as owner with full dominion or right

Omission: omitting or refusing to do, sin acts of not doing what should have been done

Peace Offering: sacrifice to bring harmony between two parties; wholesome of life

Perfect: healthy, mature, something that functions the way it was intended to function; finished, that which has reached its end

Plumb line: God's measuring standard for justice and righteous

Priesthood: office or act of a priest, Christians called by God to offer spiritual sacrifices

Righteousness: justice, upright, the approval of God, conformity to God's standard

Ruach Hakodesh: (Hebraic) wind, breath, power, Holy Spirit, invisible, immaterial, indwelling revelation of divine presence, Spirit of holiness

Sacrifice: to offer up to a higher purpose, act of worship

Sensuality: quality of being pleasing to the senses of the flesh

Sin: missing the mark, rebelliousness, disobedience, defiance, moral failing

Sinner: sinful, devoted to sin, stained, missing the mark

Sons of God: children of God heeding the leading of his Spirit, rulers of God by the Spirit

Sonship: adoption through the blood of Christ, heir of God, likeness

Spiritual: relating to the realm of the Spirit, profitable, governed by the Spirit of God

Strongman: powerful commander, dictator, stands by ready to unleash force to accomplish assignment

Transgression: to willfully disregard, rebellion, arrogant, breaking of God's law

Treason: spiritual conspiracy, disloyalty

Trespass: a false step, a falling away, lapse from truth, to slip

Unfruitful: unproductive, profitless, not of faith

Unspiritual: godless, misgoverned, worldly, unfit to access God, apart not of faith

Worshiper: seekers of God and doers of his will

Worship: to bow down before, expression of profound reverence, to adore, honor

Yahweh: (Hebraic) God of Isaac, Abraham and Jacob, YHWH (Yod Heh Vav Heh), to be, Covenant keeper, ABBA, Father, I AM

Yeshua HaMashiach: (Hebraic), Messiah, the Anointed One, the name of the Savor, Jesus Christ

OTHER BOOKS BY THE AUTHOR

BOOK ORDER INFORMATION
ONLINE @ AMAZON.COM | AUTHORHOUSE.COM

Available Formats: Hardcover, Softcover & eBook

Powerful Teaching and Deliverance Manuals
Equipping the Body of Christ For Such A Time As Time

Yeshua Ha-Moshiach

Ambassadors4Christ

Printed in the United States
By Bookmasters